Living with Disability in Canada: An Economic Portrait

by Gail Fawcett, PhD

Human Resources Development Canada

Office for Disability Issues

Développement des ressources humaines Canada

Bureau de la condition des personnes handicapées

Canadian Cataloguing in Publication Data
    Fawcett, Gail
    Living with disability in Canada : an economic portrait

    Also issued in French under title: Vivre avec une incapacité au Canada.
    Includes bibliographical references.
    ISBN 0-88810-451-0

1. Handicapped—Canada—Economic conditions.
2. Handicapped—Employment—Canada. 3. Handicapped
—Education—Canada. I. Canada. Office for Disability Issues
II. Canadian Council on Social Development III. Title
HD7256.C3F39 1996   305.9'0816'0971   C96-900742-6

Produced on behalf of Human Resources Development Canada
by: Canadian Council on Social Development
    441 MacLaren, 4th Floor
    Ottawa, Ontario K2P 2H3

Published by:
    Office for Disability Issues
    Human Resources Development Canada
    25 Eddy Street
    Hull, Quebec K1A 0J9

For additional copies, or an alternative format, please contact:
    Enquiries Centre
    Human Resources Development Canada
    140 Promenade du Portage
    Phase IV, Level O
    Hull, Quebec K1A 0J9
    Fax: (819) 953-7260

    Catalogue No. SDDP-020-10-96E
    ©Minister of Supply and Services Canada 1996
    Cat. No.: MP80-2/8-1996E
    ISBN: 0-662-25110-5

Table of Contents

Chapter 3
In the labour force

Chapter 6
Women with disabilities:
Progress in the labour market
and the domestic labour challenge . . . 151

Foreword

O ver the last 15 years, research has helped us to develop an understanding of the diverse conditions that create a handicap for persons with disabilities, whether those conditions be of a socio-political, programmatic, environmental, or attitudinal nature.

While the nature of the Canadian federation is in motion, the relationship between governments, individuals and groups is changing. The timing is right to gather and analyze the most up-to-date information on disability in Canada. This information is intended to be used as a tool in the debate about public policy on disability issues.

Dr. Gail Fawcett of the Centre for International Statistics at the Canadian Council on Social Development has dedicated her energy and talent to this tremendous task. Dr. Fawcett has produced a well-documented book which builds on *An Economic Profile of Persons With Disabilities in Canada,* (1990) by Dr. David Ross and Dr. Richard Shillington, also of the CCSD. In this book, Dr. Fawcett has also reviewed other researchers' work and the latest available data to arrive at a unique understanding of the economic circumstances of persons with disabilities in Canada. She brings evidence to light that challenges some of the persisting myths about persons with disabilities.

This book will help policy-makers to develop programs which reflect a renewed belief that persons with disabilities cannot easily be labelled as "unemployable." A single description of disability does not account for the multitude of circumstances that each individual faces. *Living with Disability in Canada* will no doubt become an essential reference for researchers, policy-makers, and all those who have an interest in contributing to an open and inclusive society.

OFFICE FOR DISABILITY ISSUES

BUREAU DE LA CONDITION DES PERSONNES HANDICAPÉES

Acknowledgements

This book could not have been written without the assistance and support of a number of individuals and organizations.

The Office for Disability Issues provided the funding for this project. It also provided assistance in the form of two dedicated individuals – Marie Lemieux and Michel Regnaud – whose input was invaluable. Marie and Michel spent many hours reviewing various drafts of this book, providing comments and suggestions, and always giving me incredible moral support. Their insight, generosity, commitment, and humour made the book possible. It was a pleasure and a privilege to work with them.

Special recognition also goes to Vivian Shalla at the Canadian Council on Social Development (CCSD) for her review of the book. Vivian's comments and suggestions were wonderfully helpful as was her moral support. Without Vivian's assistance with a variety of other tasks connected with this project, the publication of the book might have been delayed by several months as a result of the unexpected early birth of my daughter.

Angela Gibson-Kierstead at the CCSD was responsible for the many charts that appear throughout this book. Angela's talent for always knowing the best way to present complex material was greatly appreciated.

Thanks goes to Nancy Colborne Perkins and Ellen Adelberg at the CCSD for their editorial expertise and organization of the production process, as well as to Doreen Lint for the desktopping. Appreciation also goes to the following individuals from the CCSD for their comments on various portions of the book: Susan Carter, Richard Shillington, David Ross, Susan Scruton, and Laura Buckland.

The assistance of people from Statistics Canada – those connected with the HALS and Mike Sivyer (LMAS) – was much appreciated. Thanks also goes to Nancy Lawand, now the Director of CPP Program Direction, for getting the ball rolling on this project. The Canadian Society for the International Classification of Impairments, Disabilities and Handicaps and the Quebec Committee on the International Classification of Impairments, Disabilities and Handicaps deserve recognition and appreciation for developing the model of the handicaps creation process that is used throughout the book.

Finally, I would like to thank my family for their understanding and support throughout the research and writing of this book. To my parents, Claire and Dan Eno, I owe an enormous debt of gratitude for their encouragement and many hours of free childcare. Appreciation also goes to my little boy, Andrew, for understanding that Mommy had to devote all those extra hours to "The Book." And, although her early arrival presented a few scheduling problems, I would also like to thank my new baby daughter, Claire, for being so well-behaved that I was able to add the finishing touches to the book while she slept peacefully by my side.

Gail Fawcett

Chapter 1

Introduction

According to Statistics Canada's Health and Activity
Limitation Survey, about 17.8 per cent of Canada's adult
population (aged 15 and over) had some form of disability in
1991. This book provides an analysis of the economic
circumstances of those 3.8 million adult Canadians who had
a disability in that year.[1] In doing so, it also tells a story of
tremendous challenges, some successes and untapped
potential.

A number of commonly held misconceptions about
persons with disabilities are exposed. One of the main
misconceptions challenged in this book relates to the notion
of the "unemployability" of persons with disabilities. The
"employability" of persons with disabilities has as much to do
with their environment as it does with their disabilities.
Moreover, both environments and disabilities change over
time. In this book, the model used is that proposed by the
Canadian Society for the International Classification of
Impairments, Disabilities and Handicaps (CSICIDH) and the

---

1. In 1991, there were 4.2 million Canadians of all ages (15.5 per cent
of the population) with disabilities.

Quebec Committee on the International Classification of Impairments, Disabilities and Handicaps (QCICIDH), which situates disability in a wider framework. In this model, a disability interacts with environmental factors to produce a handicap situation. It is the handicap situation, not the disability in and of itself, that determines whether or not a person is employable.

In this book, Chapters 2 to 4 examine the labour force challenges of working-age adults with disabilities, as well as the hidden potential for their paid employment. Between 1986 and 1991, persons with disabilities made some significant inroads into the labour market. Labour force participation (the percentage either employed or unemployed) for this population increased during this period from about 49 per cent to about 56 per cent. However, the picture is not entirely rosy. Persons with disabilities continue to face significant barriers in their environment that inhibit many of them from reaching their full potential.

Chapter 5 provides an overview of the various income sources of all adults with disabilities and looks at poverty within that population. Finally, the unique impact of the domestic labour challenge on the economic opportunities and security of women with disabilities is the focus of Chapter 6.

In 1990, a void in the literature on disability in Canada was filled by the publication of a report entitled *An Economic Profile of Persons with Disabilities in Canada.*[2] Based on data from the 1986 Health and Activity Limitation Survey, the report utilized detailed information gathered specifically to provide comprehensive material on persons with disabilities in this country. The major source of the information presented in this current book was the 1991 Health and Activity Limitation Survey. It was not intended to replicate the earlier work, but rather to use it as a springboard and point of comparison for changes that took place between 1986 and 1991. The aim was to ask and

2.   Ross and Shillington, 1990.

answer questions that go beyond the descriptive, in order to better understand the complex interplay of factors which affect the economic security and untapped potential of Canadians with disabilities.

This book does not provide basic descriptive information about persons with disabilities; such information is readily available from a number of other sources. For example, *Persons with Disabilities*, a supplementary paper to *Improving Social Security in Canada*, presents a valuable overview of persons with disabilities in Canada in the context of social security reform.[3] Also, three publications have been produced by Statistics Canada which contain descriptive statistics using the 1991 Health and Activity Limitation Survey. These are: *Adults with Disabilities: Their Employment and Education Characteristics, Selected Characteristics of Persons with Disabilities Residing in Households*, and *A Portrait of Persons with Disabilities*.[4] An article published in *Canadian Social Trends*, "Employment of People with Disabilities," provides an overview of the labour force situation of persons with disabilities.[5] And, of a more technical nature, there is *Sources of Income of Persons with Disabilities in Canada*, a study prepared for the Employment Equity Data Program at Statistics Canada.[6]

Before proceeding, it is important to discuss the meaning of the term "disability" and explain how disability is measured in the data used in this book.

What is a disability?

While the meaning of the term "disability" may seem obvious, a great deal of confusion can be avoided by clarifying the concept. Many people have different ideas about what constitutes a disability. Some might think of a

---

3. Human Resources Development Canada, 1994.
4. See Statistics Canada, 1993b, 1994 and 1995.
5. Shain, 1995.
6. Hum and Simpson, 1994.

disability as a specific medical condition. Others might think of it in terms of a disadvantage that is created in certain situations. In fact, both of these definitions represent related concepts in the framework of the International Classification of Impairments, Disabilities and Handicaps (ICIDH). Under the original ICIDH model,[7] disability is part of a process that begins with an underlying cause and could end with a handicap. The succession of levels in this process is as follows:

underlying causes→impairments→ disabilities→handicaps

An underlying cause is typically a disease or a trauma. An impairment is an abnormality of body structure or organic function. Disabilities are functional limitations due to impairments. Handicaps are disadvantages experienced by the interaction of impairments or disabilities with an individual's surroundings. It is important to keep in mind that not all individuals will proceed through all the levels from disease or trauma to handicap. Some diseases and traumas, for example, do not lead to impairments, some impairments do not create disabilities, and some disabilities do not result in handicaps. It is not always easy to separate these concepts in one's mind, and this, no doubt, has contributed greatly to the diversity of ideas regarding the definition of disability among the general population.

This book relies on a revised version of this model which was put forth by the CSICIDH and QCICIDH. This revised version differs from the original ICIDH model by adding an extra dimension, which is the individual's "environment." In this new framework, disabilities (and impairments) interact with an individual's environment to create a handicap. The revised model can be visualized as in Figure 1.1.

---

7.   World Health Organization, 1980.

Using one of the examples provided by the CSICIDH and QCICIDH to demonstrate this model,[8] we can consider the situation of a four-year-old boy with cerebral palsy who was being integrated into a regular daycare centre. The boy was exposed to a risk factor at birth when deprived of oxygen. This "underlying cause" resulted in an impairment of his cerebral cortex, which in turn led to an additional impairment of his skeletal system – curvature of the spine. These impairments resulted in a number of disabilities – difficulty in speaking and moving about, and an inability to control defecation.

In this particular case, there were a number of environmental factors to consider. An important one was the low priority given to the integration of children with disabilities into regular daycare centres. The low priority in this case was due to a lack of financial resources. As a

Figure 1.1

Handicaps creation process

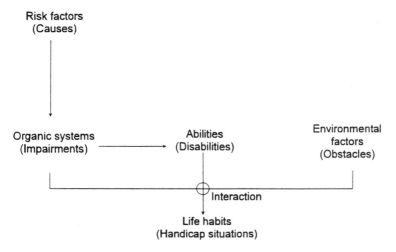

Source: Canadian Society for the International Classification of Impairments, Disabilities and Handicaps, *ICIDH International Network*, 1991, Vol.4, No.1-2: 17.

---

8. Canadian Society for the International Classification of Impairments, Disabilities and Handicaps, and Quebec Committee on the International Classification of Impairments, Disabilities and Handicaps, 1991.

result, not all of the furniture, games or activities were accessible to a child in a wheelchair. Another critical environmental factor was the attitude of the staff at the daycare centre. While the attitudes of the centre's owners and of other children had been very positive regarding children with disabilities, the staff tended to be more reserved because of the extra work involved and the lack of resource support in the community.

These environmental factors interacted with the child's disabilities to create at least two handicap situations. The child's disabilities, combined with the inaccessibility of some of the furniture, games and activities, resulted in a handicap for the child with respect to accomplishing some "life habits at the preschool education level." The attitude of the staff, combined with the child's disabilities, produced a handicap situation which affected the child's "accomplishment of life habits in the area of social relations."

In another environment, however, these handicaps could have been even more severe. Although some of the furniture, games and activities were not accessible to a child in a wheelchair, the centre itself was. Without such an environment, there would have been no chance for the child to integrate into the regular daycare centre. Moreover, the boy had been provided with technical aids which allowed non-oral communication. This meant that, although the boy had a speaking disability, he did not face a handicap in communicating. As noted in a document of the Council of Europe:

> For every handicapped person there is a corresponding handicapping situation... Handicap is not a constant but changes, resulting from the continuous interaction between the person and the objective situation.[9]

9. Chapireau, 1992, p. 8.

In this revised model, there is also room for a person to have an impairment that does not lead to a disability, but which, when coupled with environmental factors, does result in a handicap. An example of such a situation would be a person who has had a traffic accident (the underlying cause), which has resulted in facial disfigurement (the impairment), but not in a functional limitation (no disability). Coupled with the attitudes of society toward the person's appearance (environmental factors), however, this disfigurement could result in a limited set of opportunities in social situations and the workplace (the handicaps).

This is the model used throughout this publication as a basic framework to define and locate disability.

Measurement techniques used in this book

Besides the distinctions between disability and other levels in the ICIDH framework, there are a variety of ways in which disability is actually measured in surveys. This variation is due to the fact that different surveys ask different "screening questions." In this book, the primary data source is the 1991 Health and Activity Limitation Survey (HALS), though in Chapter 4, the 1989-90 Labour Market Activity Survey (LMAS) is also utilized. While the HALS provides a much richer data source on persons with disabilities, the longitudinal LMAS allows us to look at changes over the course of two years for persons with disabilities.[10] The method of identifying persons with disabilities, however, differs slightly for the two data sources.

The Health and Activity Limitation Survey contains a series of 32 screening questions (or sub-questions) designed to detect activity limitations of individuals. Following the ICIDH definition of disability, the HALS attempts to identify "any restriction or lack (resulting from an

---

10. Longitudinal data provide information on the same individuals at two or more points in time.

impairment) of ability to perform an activity in the manner or within the range considered normal for a human being."[11] The screening questions cover a number of specific activities grouped into several general ability/disability types. For example, individuals are asked if they "have any difficulty hearing what is said in a conversation with one other person" and if the difficulty has lasted or is expected to last six months or more.[12] This is one of the questions used to identify hearing disabilities. (A complete list of questions organized by disability type is contained in Appendix A.)

The seven disability types identified by the HALS are:

- hearing disabilities
- seeing disabilities
- speaking disabilities
- agility disabilities
- mobility disabilities
- mental/learning disabilities[13]
- physical disabilities not elsewhere classified (unknown)

Each question probes for an individual's difficulty in performing a particular activity. A single positive response to any of the questions results in the person being classified in the HALS as having a disability. Some people, of course, have more than one type of disability. In fact, some disability types tend to cluster together. For example, speaking disabilities are often associated with mental/learning disabilities and agility disabilities with mobility disabilities. The only mutually exclusive category of disability is the "unknown" category, which represents persons who did not

---

11. World Health Organization, 1980, p. 28.
12. HALS Questionnaire, question A1.
13. While this category includes mental, intellectual, emotional and learning disabilities, it is shortened to "mental/learning disabilities" throughout this book and to "mental disability" in graphics and tables to save space. Nonetheless, there is a great deal of variation in the nature of the disabilities represented by this disability type.

answer yes to any of the questions designed to identify hearing, seeing, speaking, agility, mobility or mental/learning disabilities, but did answer yes to at least one of the following:

> Because of a long-term physical condition or health problem, that is, one that has lasted or is expected to last six months or more, are you limited in the kind or amount of activity you can do . . .
>
> - at home?
> - at school?
> - at work?
> - in other activities, such as travel, sport or leisure?

This more general question on physical limitation demonstrates the difficulty in gathering survey information which isolates the disability level as defined by the ICIDH. While the question does inquire about activity limitations (which is equivalent to the concept of disability in the overall framework used here), it also suggests that environmental factors are an important determinant. The specific reference to work, school and home shows the importance of the setting in which the difficulty is experienced. For this reason, these screening questions might also identify handicap, since a handicap depends not only on the functional limitation, but on the setting in which that limitation is experienced.[14]

While this research relies mainly on the 1991 HALS, it is supplemented in Chapter 4 by the 1989-90 LMAS. The LMAS uses a sub-set of the HALS screening questions and identifies almost the same population. The LMAS includes 19 of the screening questions used in the HALS.[15] This sub-set identifies the same basic population of persons with

---

14. See McDowell, 1988, for a similar conclusion regarding this question on the 1986 HALS.
15. Notes in Appendix A identify which of the HALS questions were also included in the LMAS.

disabilities as the HALS and yields very similar findings. The unique contribution of the LMAS to this study is that it provides data for the same individuals over the course of two years and allows us to look at changes in disability status during that period.

As we have seen, the distinction between disability and either impairment or handicap can be difficult to grasp or measure. But while these difficulties are important to keep in mind when moving from one data source to another and when interpreting results, they are not cause for great concern about the value of the information generated. For those questions which tend to probe for handicap, it should be remembered that impairment or disability would have preceded handicap. Therefore, any question which identifies a handicap also identifies an impairment or a disability.

Focus on adults

Of the 4.2 million Canadians of all ages with disabilities in 1991, the vast majority – about 91 per cent – were adults (aged 15 and over).[16] This study concentrates on this majority.

The economic situation of children with disabilities is an important topic that warrants a separate study.[17] An economic profile of children with disabilities might address at least two main areas of inquiry. First, establishing the nature of the link between the economic resources of families and the incidence of disability among children in those families would be very useful in understanding the true impact of poverty and assessing the progress of Canada's socio-economic programs. Second, information on the barriers and costs faced by families with children who have disabilities is necessary for us to appreciate the enormous

---

16. As a result of data availability, this study is also limited to adults living in households; the vast majority of adults with disabilities live in households.

17. The microdata tapes of the HALS 1991 Children's Survey and Institutions Survey have not been released to the public.

economic contribution made by such families. It would also help to assess the potential for great inequality of opportunity for children with disabilities living in families with fewer economic resources. These questions are matters for future research and go beyond the scope of this book.[18]

Presentation of the data

Unless otherwise stated, all 1991 figures were generated by the author using Statistics Canada's microdata tape of the 1991 HALS for adults in households. All 1986 figures were recalculated by the author using data from *An Economic Profile of Persons with Disabilities in Canada* or from Statistics Canada's *The Daily* (July 27, 1993).

In the present analysis, all "not stated" categories were eliminated for ease of presentation and understanding. In some instances, numbers were drawn from *An Economic Profile* and *The Daily* in order to provide a point of comparison to 1986. However, tables that appeared in those two documents typically included the additional "not stated" category, which contained individuals who failed to provide answers to specific questions. To maintain consistency, 1986 figures taken from *An Economic Profile* and *The Daily* that appear in this book were recalculated to exclude the "not stated" category and, therefore, may not match exactly the figures contained in those reports.

In some instances, figures in this book do not include persons who were living in the Northwest Territories or the Yukon, since data on this portion of the population were not released on the microdata tape for specific questions. This includes any figures containing age breakdowns or poverty rates.

---

18. For more general information on children with disabilities, see: *The Health of Canada's Children* (Canadian Institute of Child Health, 1994); *Children and Youth with Disabilities in Canada* by Denise Avard (Canadian Institute of Child Health, 1994); "Children with Disabilities" by Katherine Nessner in *Canadian Social Trends* (No. 19, Winter, 1990); and "Disabilities Among Children" by Jillian Oderkirk in *Canadian Social Trends* (No. 31, Winter, 1993).

All figures that provide information on requirements for special workplace accommodations exclude persons who were self-employed or working without pay in a family business.

All numbers in this publication have been rounded to the nearest thousand. As a result, some of the column totals in the tables may not add up to the totals listed. All totals were obtained by adding non-rounded numbers, then rounding the total.

Most of the data presented here pertain to persons aged 15 to 64, and unless otherwise stated, tables and charts apply only to this age group. Some of the tables and charts presented in Chapters 5 and 6 include information on persons aged 65 and older and have been labelled as such.

Labour force participants are those who were either employed or unemployed but actively seeking work. The unemployment rate is the percentage of all those participating in the labour force who were unemployed. Poverty rates are based on Statistics Canada's Low Income Cut-offs, as explained in Chapter 5.

Much of the data presented in the main body of this book is summarized graphically throughout. Readers may find supporting tables for selected items in Appendix B.

Organization of this book

Chapters 2 through 4 concentrate on the working-age population of persons with disabilities (aged 15 to 64). Chapter 5 contains a more global look at income sources and poverty among adults of all ages with disabilities. Finally, Chapter 6 examines the impact of domestic labour on the economic security of women with disabilities. The following is a brief summary of these chapters.

Chapter 2, *Getting into the labour force: The participation of persons with disabilities*, examines the factors associated with the participation of persons with disabilities in the labour force. Higher education, for example, appears to be one of the most valuable mechanisms available to mitigate the difficulty persons with disabilities face in trying to get into and stay in the paid labour market. Increases in the educational attainment of the working-age population of persons with disabilities between 1986 and 1991 may be responsible for about a third of the overall increase in their participation rate during that period.

Environmental factors also seem to have an effect on the labour force participation of persons with disabilities. One's living arrangements have a notable impact, for example. Persons with disabilities who live alone have significantly lower rates of participation than those who live with others. Participation rates also vary by age and sex, with the oldest age group (55 to 64) and women having lower rates. The combination of being older and a woman leads to the lowest rates of participation of all. Women with disabilities, however, began to narrow the participation gap between 1986 and 1991. In particular, the participation rate of younger women with disabilities increased at a faster pace than that of men.

Chapter 2 also investigates certain aspects of the disability itself (severity, type and cause), which have a significant effect on labour force participation rates. Persons with mild disabilities have much higher rates than those with severe disabilities. The greatest gains in participation between 1986 and 1991 were among those with mild disabilities; this resulted in a widening of the participation gap between those with mild and those with severe disabilities. Both the type of disability and the cause of disability are also related to participation rates. However, in both cases, differences in severity explain much of this variation.

In spite of the connection with severity, type and cause of disability affect labour force participation rates independently. For example, regardless of severity, people with either hearing or unknown physical disabilities have higher rates of participation than those with other types of disabilities; and those with disabilities that have a work-related cause also have higher rates of participation than those with disabilities due to other causes.

Chapter 3, *In the labour force: Successes and challenges*, presents a profile of persons with disabilities participating in the labour force. These individuals face unusually high rates of unemployment. Once they secure employment, however, it is likely to be full-time. Moreover, the earnings gap between persons with and without disabilities is not as large as one might expect, given the disadvantages that persons with disabilities face trying to enter the labour force. The greatest hurdle they face seems to be simply finding a job. For those who do find a job, education is probably the most important determinant of earnings. People with higher levels of education are more likely to have work-related training and to be employed in some of the more lucrative occupations.

Some groups with disabilities, however, are more disadvantaged in the labour force than others. For example, women, youth and persons with mental/learning or speaking disabilities experience higher levels of unemployment and lower levels of earnings.

Chapter 4, *Out of the labour force: Untapped potential*, focusses on persons with disabilities of working age who were not participating in the paid labour force. There is ample evidence of both a willingness and ability to work among this population. Many persons with disabilities are outside of the labour force, not because their disability prevents them from working, but because the labour market is an environment that produces handicap situations. More than half of those with disabilities who were out of the labour force either indicated some obvious sign of future work potential (such as the intention to look for work) or reported that they were prevented from looking for work because of environmental barriers. In addition, there appears to be a significant change in people's disability status from year to year. Many disabilities are cyclical in nature, and therefore their impact on one's labour force activity varies over time. Changes in both environmental factors and the disabilities themselves can result in a tremendous flux in labour force activity from year to year.

Labour force participation is only one aspect of the overall economic profile. Chapter 5, *Income sources and low income among persons with disabilities*, offers a wider look at the economic portrait. Adults with disabilities are more likely to be poor than those without disabilities. Source of income is a key factor in determining whether or not persons with disabilities will live in poverty. Those who have earnings from employment are less likely to be poor than those who receive social assistance, for example. As well, the disability income support system in Canada is made up of a fragmented collection of programs, which leads to a great variation in poverty rates among those who rely on different programs.

As noted throughout this book, there are often significant differences in the economic situation of women and men with disabilities. Chapter 6, *Women with disabilities: Progress in the labour market and the domestic labour challenge,* includes a discussion of the impact of domestic labour on women and men with disabilities. Those who have some assistance with domestic chores, such as meal preparation and everyday housework, are more likely to participate in the labour force. However, women and men are not equally likely to have such assistance. Women with disabilities are much more likely than their male counterparts to perform household chores alone. Men with disabilities receive far more assistance with such chores, regardless of the severity of their disability.

Only young women, aged 15 to 24, have a significant level of assistance with household chores. These young women also have much higher levels of education and their labour force participation rates are very close to those of their male counterparts. At this stage, it is not clear whether these young women represent a unique cohort in history or are simply at a phase of their life cycle where the domestic labour challenge has yet to have a significant impact upon them.

Throughout this book, it becomes clear that persons with disabilities face countless economic challenges. Perhaps one of the greatest hurdles is finding an employer willing to consider *abilities* rather than *disabilities*. The following chapters provide a look at the complexity of factors that influence the economic circumstances of persons with disabilities.

Chapter 2

Getting into the labour force:
The participation of persons with disabilities

This chapter examines a range of factors affecting participation in the labour force by people with disabilities. This is a crucial subject of investigation because earnings from employment represent the most important source of income for adults with disabilities. More than 60 per cent of the working-age population with disabilities had employment earnings in 1991, and these earnings represented nearly three-quarters of all income received by adults under the age of 65 with disabilities.[1] Earnings also lessened an individual's likelihood of living in poverty.

The first step toward earning an income from employment is to be able to participate in the labour force. Those who participate in the labour force are those who are either employed or unemployed and seeking work. Persons with disabilities face special challenges when attempting to

1. Statistics Canada, 1995, p. 61.

enter the labour market. These challenges often go beyond
the disability itself. Environmental barriers can transform a
disability into a handicap and force unemployed persons
with disabilities into the ranks of the "hidden unemployed."
These are individuals who would prefer to have paid
employment, but have become so discouraged by
unemployment that they have stopped looking for work.

The first section of this chapter provides an overview of
the labour force participation rates of persons with
disabilities, including a comparison of those with disabilities
and those without. It also looks at some of the changes that
took place between 1986 and 1991. The remaining sections
examine some of the factors which appear to affect
participation rates among persons with disabilities. In some
instances, these factors are best described as the
characteristics or circumstances of individuals, including
sex, age, level of education and living arrangements. In
other instances, these factors are characteristics of the
disabilities, including the type of disability, its cause and its
severity.

Overview of labour force participation rates (1986 and 1991)

The labour force participation rate for persons without
disabilities increased very slightly from 78 per cent in 1986
to 80.9 per cent in 1991.[2] However, this slight increase in
overall participation rates fails to capture some significant
sex-related changes that have occurred in the general
population (among persons with and without disabilities)
since the early 1960s. For men in the general population,
the participation rate has been declining rather steadily,
largely because of an increasing trend toward early

2.   Figures for 1986 were calculated using numbers provided in
     Statistics Canada's *The Daily*, July 27, 1993. The percentages
     appearing in *The Daily* included the "not stated" category. In order
     to provide consistency for the 1986-1991 comparison, therefore,
     percentages for 1986 were recalculated to exclude the "not stated"
     category using the numbers in *The Daily*.

retirement. However, since the early 1960s, women have entered the labour force in increasing numbers. In 1990 this trend for women in general began to slow down considerably as the country entered a period of economic recession.[3]

Persons with and without disabilities: the participation gap narrows

Historically, the labour force participation rate of persons with disabilities has been lower than that of persons without disabilities. Between 1986 and 1991, however, the participation gap began to narrow (Figure 2.1). While the labour force participation of persons without disabilities increased slightly, the rate among persons with disabilities increased even more, from 48.5 per cent in 1986 to 56.3 per cent in 1991. In 1986, the participation rate of persons with disabilities was 62.2 per cent of that for persons without disabilities; by 1991, this had increased to 69.6 per cent.

Figure 2.1

Labour force participation rates*of persons with and without disabilities, 1986 and 1991

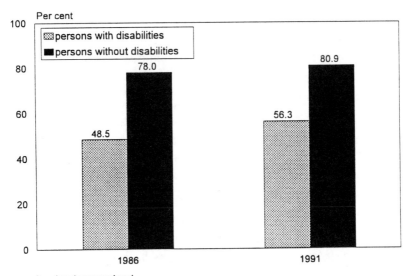

*employed or unemployed
See "Presentation of data" in Chapter 1 for assumptions used.

3. Basset, 1994.

Seemingly undaunted by the economic restructuring taking place during the late 1980s, an increasing proportion of persons with disabilities demonstrated their willingness and ability to participate in the paid labour force. It is impossible to determine exactly what might have caused this increase in labour force participation, but a number of factors discussed below may have contributed.

Government and non-government initiatives

The increase in labour force participation among persons with disabilities coincided with a number of government initiatives, and with a period of heightened awareness fuelled by the "disability movement" itself. Some federal government initiatives during this period included:

- the establishment of the Status of Disabled Persons Secretariat in 1985, which was put in place to increase awareness about issues related to disability and support the participation of persons with disabilities in society;

- the *Employment Equity Act* of 1986, which applies to Crown corporations and federally regulated employers (having at least 100 employees) and requires that these employers identify and eliminate employment barriers for four designated groups – women, Aboriginal peoples, members of visible minority groups and persons with disabilities;

- the Federal Contractors Program of 1986, which required contractors to the federal government (with more than 100 employees and bidding on contracts of over $200,000) to remove barriers that might restrict the hiring, promotion and training of persons with disabilities within their organization;

- the 1988 amendment to the *National Transportation Act*, designed to increase the accessibility of federal modes of transportation to persons with disabilities.

In addition to these government initiatives, issues surrounding persons with disabilities were brought to the forefront through a number of other avenues, among them:

- the publicity generated by the United Nations Decade of Disabled Persons (1982-1991);

- the spread of the independent living movement across the country during the mid to late 1980s;[4]

- the efforts of disability groups working actively to raise awareness and create change at community and national levels.

All of these activities likely aided the entry of persons with disabilities into the paid labour force, although their exact impact is impossible to assess. We do know that a number of individual success stories give credit to particular programs. However, recent attempts to assess the effectiveness of certain programs reveal some concerns. For example, the *Report of the Standing Committee on Human Rights and the Status of Disabled Persons* voiced a concern that federal employment programs have lacked a "strategic framework for dealing with disability-related issues"[5] and that "there has been little done to improve the participation rate of persons with disabilities in departmental employment programming."[6]

An increasing proportion with mild disabilities

Between 1986 and 1991, the proportion of persons with disabilities classified as mild as opposed to moderate or severe increased. There has been some speculation that the increase in participation is largely due to the higher proportion of persons with milder disabilities (from 51.6 per cent of working-age persons with disabilities in 1986, to 54.3 per cent in 1991). As discussed later in this chapter, persons

---

4. The independent living movement "is typically defined as control over one's life based on choice of acceptable options that minimize reliance on others in organizing and performing everyday activities." Boschen, 1995, p. 1.

5. Report of the Standing Committee on Human Rights and the Status of Disabled Persons, 1995, pp. 14-15.

6. Ibid., p. 15.

with mild disabilities are more likely to be in the paid labour force than those with moderate or severe disabilities. How much of the increase in labour force participation of all persons with disabilities was due to this shift in severity level between 1986 and 1991? The evidence available from the 1986 and 1991 HALS data suggests that only about 10 per cent of the actual increase in labour force participation rates for all working-age persons with disabilities was due to the increase in the proportion of those with mild disabilities.[7]

Increasing levels of educational attainment

Increasing levels of education among persons with disabilities between 1986 and 1991 also contributed to their increased rate of labour force participation. As discussed later in this chapter, the overall levels of educational attainment for working-age persons with disabilities were higher in 1991 than in 1986. How much of the increase in labour force participation might have been due to these increased levels of educational attainment? The evidence available from the 1986 and 1991 HALS data suggests that more than one-third of the increased participation rate between 1986 and 1991 was likely due to increased

---

7.   A simple exercise can be used to estimate the proportion of the increased participation rate that might be attributed to changes in severity level alone. As we learn later in this chapter, changes occurred in the participation rates within each severity level as well as the above-mentioned changes in the proportion of persons in each severity level. In this exercise, I begin by estimating what the overall participation rate would have been in 1991 if only the proportion of persons in each severity level had changed (that is, assuming participation rates within each severity level remained at the 1986 level). The overall participation rate of all persons with disabilities in 1991 would have been 49.3 per cent if there had been no change in participation rates within each severity level (only changes in the proportion of persons in each severity level). In fact, the actual participation rate of all working-age persons with disabilities rose from 48.5 per cent in 1986 to 56.3 per cent in 1991 (a difference of 7.8 percentage points). This means that changes in the proportion of persons in each severity level alone would have accounted for only 10.3 per cent. This is calculated as follows:
       49.3 (estimated 1991 participation rate)
     - 48.5 (actual 1986 participation rate)
        .8 (estimated percentage point increase)
   .8 (estimated percentage point increase) divided by 7.8 (actual percentage point increase) = 10.3 per cent of the actual increase in the participation rate of all working-age persons with disabilities.

educational attainment by persons with disabilities during this period.[8]

Factors affecting labour force participation: sex and age

Two of the most significant factors affecting the labour force participation of persons with disabilities are their sex and age.

Sex and labour force participation

Participation rates in the labour force differ markedly by sex for both persons with and without disabilities. In the general population, women have historically had lower rates of participation in the labour force. However, as noted earlier, the participation gap between women and men has

---

8. Again, a simple exercise can be used to estimate the amount of the increase in the participation rate that might be attributed to changes in educational attainment. Some changes in the participation rates occurred within each level of educational attainment between 1986 and 1991, in addition to the above-mentioned changes in the proportion of persons at each level of educational attainment. (The participation rate increased slightly for most levels of educational attainment, but the largest increase was among those with incomplete post-secondary schooling.)

The first task in this exercise is to estimate what the overall participation rate would have been in 1991 if only the proportion of persons at each level of educational attainment had changed (that is, assuming participation rates within each level of educational attainment remained at the 1986 level). With these assumptions, the overall participation rate of all persons with disabilities in 1991 would have been 51.4 per cent. As noted earlier, the actual participation rate of all working-age persons with disabilities rose from 48.5 per cent in 1986 to 56.3 per cent in 1991 (a difference of 7.8 percentage points). This means that changes in the proportion of persons within each level of educational attainment alone would have accounted for about 37.2 per cent. This is calculated as follows:

  51.4 (estimated 1991 participation rate)
- 48.5 (actual 1986 participation rate)
  2.9 (estimated percentage point increase)

2.9 (estimated percentage point increase) divided by 7.8 (actual percentage point increase) = 37.2 per cent of the actual increase in the participation rate of all working-age persons with disabilities

This means that the shift in educational attainment between 1986 and 1991 is likely to have been responsible for more than one-third of the increased participation rate (all other things being equal).

narrowed over the past two decades, as women have entered the labour force in record numbers and men have increasingly entered into early retirement. Persons with disabilities also experienced this narrowing of the sex gap in participation rates between 1986 and 1991.[9]

As summarized in Figure 2.2, 37.6 per cent of working-age women with disabilities were in the labour force in 1986; by 1991, this figure had grown to 48.5 per cent, an increase of about 29 per cent (or 10.9 percentage points). For working-age men with disabilities, the participation rate

Figure 2.2

Labour force participation rates*of women and men with disabilities,1986 and 1991

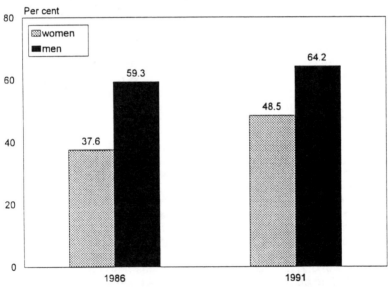

*employed or unemployed
See "Presentation of data" in Chapter 1 for assumptions used.

9.   There was, however, a significant difference between persons with and without disabilities in the manner in which the sex gap in participation narrowed. For both populations, the participation rate of women increased between 1986 and 1991. Among persons without disabilities, the participation rate of men declined during this period. Among persons with disabilities, however, the participation rate of men actually increased – it merely increased at a lower rate than for women with disabilities. Thus, the end result for both populations is an overall narrowing in the sex gap.

grew from 59.3 per cent in 1986 to 64.2 per cent in 1991, an increase of only about 8 per cent (or 4.9 percentage points).

Age and labour force participation

Age is another important factor affecting the labour force participation of persons with disabilities. As in 1986, persons aged 25 to 44 with disabilities had the highest level of participation in the paid labour force in 1991 (at 68.6 per cent) of all age groups, and those aged 45 to 64 had the lowest (at 45.1 per cent). Among all three age groups listed in Table 2.1, labour force participation (the proportion either employed or unemployed) increased between 1986 and 1991. The greatest increase was among older persons with disabilities – a 24.2 per cent increase for those aged 45 to 64, although they also had the lowest rate of participation of the three groups listed. Young people (aged 15 to 24) with disabilities were also much more likely to be in the labour force in 1991 than in 1986 (a 15.8 per cent increase), as were those aged 25 to 44, but the increase for the latter group was less marked.

Table 2.1

Labour force participation rates* of persons with disabilities by age, 1986 and 1991

Age	1986 %	1991 %	% Increase	1991 Number
15-24	53.9	62.4	15.8	262,000
25-44	65.4	68.6	4.9	892,000
45-64	36.3	45.1	24.2	1,136,000
Total	**48.4**	**56.2**	**16.1**	**2,290,000**

*employed or unemployed
See "Presentation of data" in Chapter 1 for assumptions used.

Persons aged 45 to 64 with disabilities had the lowest
rate of labour force participation of any age group in both
1986 and 1991. However, this group registered the highest
rate of increase in participation between 1986 and 1991.
This increase among persons aged 45 to 64 with disabilities
stands in curious contrast to the trend toward early
retirement for this same age group in the general population.
It is possible that the people aged 45 to 64 with disabilities in
1991 were better educated than their 1986 contemporaries.
This could have resulted in the increased participation, since
there is a positive relationship between education and
labour force participation. It is also quite likely that the age
distribution within this category changed slightly between
1986 and 1991. Due to the effects of the "baby boom"
generation, in 1991 more of that category were aged 45 to
54 (before the typical age for early retirement).
Nevertheless, there are a host of other possible
explanations for these findings, none of which can be
confirmed here.

Including all people between the ages of 45 and 64 in
one group obscures some interesting information with
respect to participation rates (although this is not the case
for those aged 25 to 44). The age groups presented in Table
2.1 allow for direct points of comparison between 1986 and
1991, as these were the age breakdowns used in *An
Economic Profile of Persons with Disabilities in Canada.*[10]
However, an additional age breakdown is presented in the
next section to highlight some of the important differences
within the 45 to 64 age category. This new breakdown
simply separates the 45 to 64 age category into two groups:

10. The age breakdowns originally available on the HALS public-use
     tape were as follows: 15 to 34, 35 to 54, 55 to 64 and 65 plus.
     However, it is important to be able to isolate finer age groups when
     examining economic issues. In particular, the youth group (15 to 24)
     is unique with respect to many of the questions raised in this book.
     For this reason, an additional data file was secured from Statistics
     Canada which allowed the following age breakdowns: 15 to 24, 35
     to 44, 45 to 54, 55 to 64 and 65 plus. Unfortunately, the data for the
     Northwest Territories and Yukon had been suppressed on this
     additional file. Therefore, the data presented by age breakdowns in
     this publication excludes persons in the Northwest Territories and
     Yukon.

45 to 54 and 55 to 64. To provide as much information as possible while keeping the number of categories to a minimum, the age breakdown used for the next several figures is 15 to 24 years, 25 to 44 years, 45 to 54 years and 55 to 64 years.

It is evident in Figure 2.3 that labour force participation among persons with disabilities peaked at 68.6 per cent for those between the ages of 25 and 44, declined to 61 per cent for those between the ages of 45 and 54 and dropped to a low of 32.2 per cent among 55 to 64-year-olds. A similar pattern was found among persons without disabilities. Indeed, participation in the labour force among persons without disabilities also peaked between the ages of 25 and 44 (around 89 per cent), began to decline between ages 45 and 54 (85.2 per cent) and dropped significantly for those aged 55 to 64 (60.8 per cent). While the general pattern was the same for persons with and without disabilities, it is important to observe that within each age group, persons

Figure 2.3

Labour force participation rates* of persons with disabilities by age, 1991

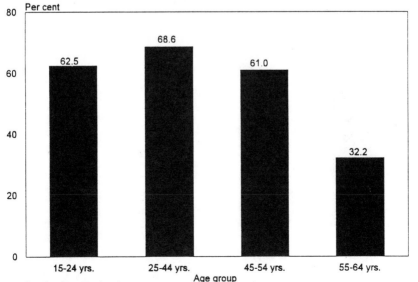

*employed or unemployed
See "Presentation of data" in Chapter 1 for assumptions used.

with disabilities had a lower level of participation and that the drop in participation between the ages of 55 and 64 was somewhat more dramatic among persons with disabilities.

It is not surprising that a fairly high proportion of persons aged 55 to 64 were "not in the labour force" (either employed or unemployed). The trend toward retirement before the age of 65 has been increasing since the 1960s.[11] Persons with disabilities may be no exception to this trend. Nonetheless, persons with disabilities and persons without disabilities are likely to have different reasons for taking early retirement and to experience differences in the economic options available to them for early retirement.

Labour force participation and the interaction of age and sex

The labour force participation gap between women and men varies according to the age group. The sex gap in

Figure 2.4

Labour force participation rates* of women and men with disabilities by age, 1991

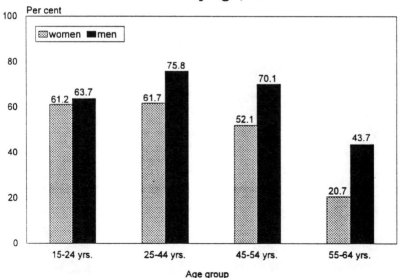

*employed or unemployed
See "Presentation of data" in Chapter 1 for assumptions used.

11. Schellenberg, 1994.

labour force participation was lowest among the younger age groups and increased steadily by age for persons with disabilities. As illustrated in Figure 2.4, the participation rate of women aged 15 to 24 with disabilities was very close to that of their male counterparts (61.2 per cent for women and 63.7 per cent for men). The participation rate of this youngest group of women with disabilities was about 96 per cent that of men.

With age, however, this gap increased. Among 25 to 44-year-olds with disabilities, the participation rate of women was 81 per cent that of men (61.7 per cent of women in the labour force compared with 75.8 per cent of men), and among those 45 to 54, this figure was down to 74 per cent (participation rate for women of 52.1 per cent and for men of 70.1 per cent). It dropped to 47 per cent among those 55 to 64 (participation rate for women of 20.7 per cent and for men of 43.7 per cent). While the combination of having a disability and being between the ages of 55 and 64 substantially reduced the likelihood of a person being in the paid labour force, being a woman further cut that likelihood in half.

Sex and participation rates for the youngest age group: excluding those still in school

Additional factors, such as school enrolment, provide us with a better understanding of the differences in labour force participation rates between young women and men aged 15 to 24. Many individuals aged 15 to 24 are still pursuing schooling, and we would not expect to find them in the labour force. Therefore, it might be more meaningful to compare the participation rates of those who were not enrolled in school.

By excluding individuals enrolled in school from the analysis, two important points become evident. First, the participation rates of both women and men aged 15 to 24 with disabilities increased noticeably (to 73.9 per cent for women and 70.5 per cent for men, according to Figure 2.5) compared to those illustrated in Figure 2.4. It becomes clear that a significant portion of 15 to 24-year-olds were not in the labour force because they were still pursuing their education.

The second important point that emerges is that the sex gap in labour force participation for 15 to 24-year-olds was reversed when students were excluded from the analysis. That is, the participation rate of young women (15 to 24) with disabilities who were not students was greater than that of their male counterparts. This suggests that a higher proportion of women than men aged 15 to 24 with disabilities were enrolled in school. In fact, almost 62 per cent of the women in this age group were enrolled in school compared with about 56 per cent of the men.[12]

Figure 2.5

Labour force participation rates* of women and men with disabilities not enrolled in school, by age, 1991

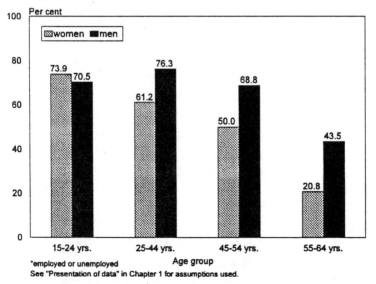

*employed or unemployed
See "Presentation of data" in Chapter 1 for assumptions used.

12. This discussion focusses on the youngest age group because there are relatively few individuals over age 24 who are still in school (between 7 and 14 per cent).

Sex and participation rates: excluding women with dependent children

Another factor which is expected to influence sex differences in labour force participation rates is the presence of dependent children in the household. Historically, the presence of dependent children has been associated with a reduction in the labour force participation rate of all women. This is because women have traditionally borne the primary responsibility for child care, with many delaying, interrupting or foregoing careers in the labour market to stay home with their children. Women with disabilities are no exception to this trend.

The role of children in the labour force participation of women with disabilities will be discussed in more detail in Chapter 6. At this point, however, one final comparison between the sexes may be useful in demonstrating how unique the 1991 labour force participation rates were for women aged 15 to 24. Figure 2.6 illustrates the participation rates of women with disabilities who did not have dependent

Figure 2.6

Labour force participation rates* of women with disabilities without dependent children at home and of men with disabilities, by age**, 1991

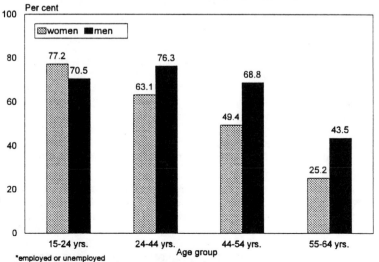

*employed or unemployed
**excludes women and men who were enrolled in school
See "Presentation of data" in Chapter 1 for assumptions used.

children and the participation rates of men by age group in 1991.[13] Women aged 15 to 24 with disabilities who did not have responsibility for childrearing participated in the labour force at an even higher rate than did men. Young women with disabilities who were neither in school nor involved in childrearing had a participation rate of 77.2 per cent (Figure 2.6), while young men with disabilities not in school had a participation rate of 70.5 per cent.

Factors affecting labour force participation: education

The level of education attained by persons with disabilities has a strong effect on their participation in the paid labour force.

Education and labour force participation[14]

Education is generally considered to enhance an individual's skill and productive potential and to increase an individual's labour force opportunities. Persons with higher levels of education have historically been more likely to participate in the paid labour force and to earn more once employment has been secured. Persons with disabilities have been no exception to this pattern. As illustrated in Figure 2.7, persons with disabilities who had the highest level of education (university) participated in the labour force

13. Women and men enrolled in school were also excluded from this analysis. The data presented here for men, however, include men with and without children. It is not possible in the HALS to identify the presence of dependent children for men. Such data exist only for women. However, since the presence of dependent children in the household historically has had a much more dramatic impact on the labour force activity of women than men, this difference in the comparison groups should not be a major problem in accurately interpreting these findings.

14. The levels of educational attainment presented here match those used in *An Economic Profile of Persons with Disabilities in Canada* to allow for direct comparison. The order in which the levels appear is based on the approximate number of years of formal education required to attain the certification in question. It should be noted, however, that trades certification often requires a prolonged period of training which takes place outside the formal education system (in the form of apprenticeship).

at almost double the rate of those with the lowest level (primary school or lower) in 1991.

As outlined earlier, the increase in educational attainment of working-age persons with disabilities between 1986 and 1991 may have been responsible for as much as a third of the total increase in their labour force participation. Figure 2.8 demonstrates that fewer working-age persons with disabilities had only the lowest levels of education in 1991, compared to 1986. In 1986, 28.9 per cent of this population had primary school education or less; in 1991, this figure was down to 19.7 per cent. As well, there were slight increases in the proportion of this population who had obtained each of the higher levels of education.

In spite of the effectiveness of education in increasing the participation of persons with disabilities in the labour force, a persistent gap remained in the participation rates of persons with and without disabilities, even for those who had the same levels of education. The gap was greatest for

Figure 2.7

Labour force participation rates* of persons with disabilities by highest level of education, 1991

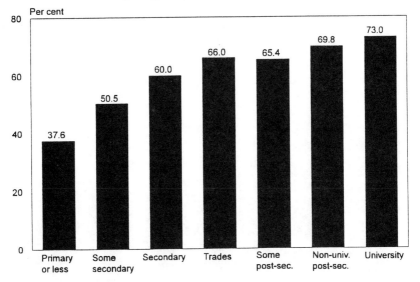

*employed or unemployed
See "Presentation of data" in Chapter 1 for assumptions used.

those with primary school education or less (Figure 2.9); in this group, persons with disabilities participated at only 59 per cent of the rate of persons without disabilities. The gap narrowed markedly among those with some secondary school education, where persons with disabilities participated at 73 per cent of the rate of persons without disabilities. From this point on, increasing levels of education closed the participation gap between persons with and without disabilities at a fairly constant and modest rate (with a slight deviation for those with trades education). The labour force participation gap was narrowest for those with university education, where persons with disabilities participated at about 80 per cent of the rate of persons without disabilities. Thus, while higher education for persons with disabilities eases their entry into the labour force and narrows the difference in participation rates compared to persons without disabilities, it cannot, by itself, eliminate the employment disadvantage stemming from the disability.

Figure 2.8
Highest level of education completed by persons with disabilities, 1986 and 1991

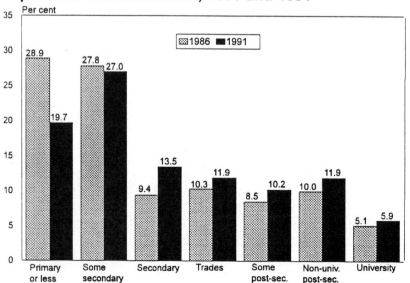

See "Presentation of data" in Chapter 1 for assumptions used.

Figure 2.9

Labour force participation rates* of persons with and without disabilities by highest level of education, 1991

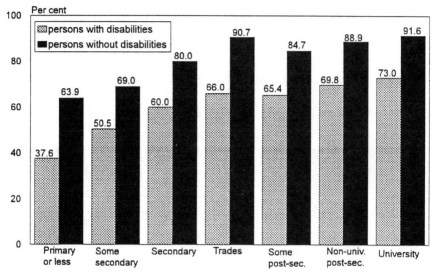

*employed or unemployed
See "Presentation of data" in Chapter 1 for assumptions used.

Time of education in relation to the onset of disability[15]

If higher education generally leads to greater labour force participation by persons with disabilities, does it make a difference whether an individual has the disability at the time she or he is pursuing that education? From the HALS data of both 1986 and 1991, it would appear so.

In *An Economic Profile of Persons with Disabilities in Canada*, it was found that in 1986, persons who had their disability before completing their education were more likely to participate in the labour market than those whose disability began after completion of education. The same

---

15. In this section, the levels of educational attainment are presented as a collapsed version (for example, non-university post-secondary and university degrees are included in one category) of the educational attainment levels presented in the previous section. This allows for ease of interpretation and ensures that the sample size is adequate for this more involved view of the relationship between participation and education.

was true in 1991. As Figure 2.10 shows, among those persons whose underlying condition began after they completed their education, 52.7 per cent were in the labour force (either employed or unemployed) in 1991. However, among those whose underlying condition was present prior to the time they completed their education, 67.9 per cent were participating in the labour force. Although it is impossible to determine the precise reasons for these differences, Ross and Shillington suggest two interpretations:

- first, that those who became disabled before completing their education were more likely to be younger, and thus to have had *more opportunity to plan ahead* and to adapt their future work lives accordingly;

- second, that recognizing the employment disadvantage of having a disability, they took steps to extend their formal education and training. [16]

Figure 2.10

Labour force participation rates* for persons with disabilities by education and whether the underlying condition was present before or after completion of education, 1991

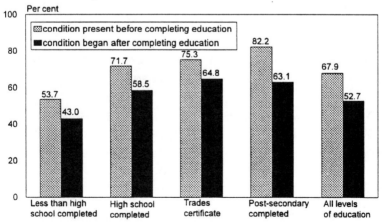

*employed or unemployed
See "Presentation of data" in Chapter 1 for assumptions used.

---

16. Ross and Shillington, 1990, p. 49.

Given the findings in the 1991 data, these interpretations seem reasonable. As summarized in Table 2.2, persons whose underlying condition was present before completing their education tended to have higher levels of education than those whose underlying condition began after they finished their schooling. About a quarter of those whose underlying condition was present while they were still in school had completed post-secondary education. On the other hand, only about 16 per cent of those whose underlying condition began after completion of schooling had post-secondary degrees or diplomas. Although not shown here, a further analysis of this information indicates that this relationship was true regardless of age. This

Table 2.2

Highest level of education of persons with disabilities, by whether the underlying condition was present before or after completion of education, 1991

Highest level of education	Condition present before completion of education	
	%	Number
Less than high school completed	38.5	178,000
High school completed	25.1	116,000
Trades certificate	10.5	49,000
Post-secondary school completed	25.9	120,000
All levels	**100.0**	**462,000**

Highest level of education	Condition began after completion of education	
	%	Number
Less than high school completed	47.8	641,000
High school completed	22.4	300,000
Trades certificate	14.0	188,000
Post-secondary school completed	15.8	212,000
All levels	**100.0**	**1,341,000**

See "Presentation of data" in Chapter 1 for assumptions used.

certainly supports Ross and Shillington's view that individuals were more likely to extend their formal education and training if the onset of their disability occurred before schooling was completed.[17]

The degree to which labour force participation was increased because a person had the underlying condition before completing school also depended upon the level of schooling attained. Persons whose disability occurred before they completed their education had a greater likelihood of being in the labour force, but the most pronounced effect was on those with post-secondary education.[18] Figure 2.10 demonstrates that individuals who had completed post-secondary education and had the underlying condition before they finished school had a labour force participation rate of 82.2 per cent, compared to a rate of 63.1 per cent for those whose disability commenced after they completed school.

Factors affecting labour force participation: living arrangements

Whether or not a person with a disability lived alone or with others was another factor that affected labour force participation. In the following section, the relationship between living alone and labour force participation is presented. This relationship is examined more fully by considering the individual's responsibility for domestic tasks.

Living arrangements and labour force participation

In the 1991 HALS data, the extent of participation in the labour force was clearly related to whether or not persons with disabilities lived alone or with others. Furthermore, the

---

17. About one-quarter of all working-age persons with disabilities had the underlying condition before completing school.

18. It is likely that choices regarding both the level and type of education are also important, but the HALS data do not allow us to examine the effects of the discipline studied.

nature of this relationship was quite different for persons with and persons without disabilities.

Among persons without disabilities, living alone was associated with higher levels of labour force participation. As illustrated in Figure 2.11, in 1991, both women and men without disabilities had higher rates of labour force participation when they lived alone. This difference was particularly pronounced for women – 82.5 per cent of women without disabilities who lived alone were in the labour force, compared to 72.7 per cent of women without disabilities who lived with others. [19]

The pattern was reversed for persons with disabilities. For both women and men with disabilities, living alone reduced their likelihood of being in the labour force. Among women with disabilities who lived alone, 43.5 per cent were in the labour force; among those who lived with others, 49.7

Figure 2.11

Labour force participation rates* for women and men with and without disabilities, by living arrangements, 1991

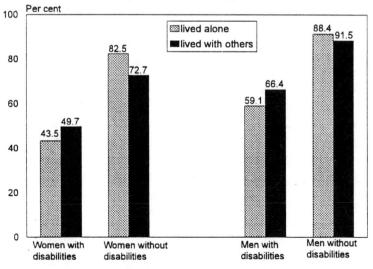

*employed or unemployed
See "Presentation of data" in Chapter 1 for assumptions used.

19. The reasons are likely related to childbearing and childrearing.

per cent were in the labour force. Similarly, 59.1 per cent of men with disabilities who lived alone participated in the labour force, while 66.4 per cent of those who lived with others were participants (Figure 2.11). For many persons with disabilities, unlike those without disabilities, living with others seemed to facilitate entry into the labour force.

It is interesting to note that persons with disabilities were also more likely than persons without disabilities to live alone. About 12 per cent of women with disabilities lived alone, compared to only 6 per cent of women without disabilities. Similarly, almost 12 per cent of men with disabilities lived alone, compared to 7 per cent of men without disabilities (not illustrated).

Living arrangements: who performs the domestic work?

For some persons with disabilities, being in the labour force (either employed or unemployed) may only be possible if they have some assistance or special accommodation. Without such assistance and accommodations, a disability can lead to a handicap and make work very difficult or impossible. The perception a person with a disability has of their ability to work may have as much to do with that individual's environment as it does with the disability. [20]

The support provided by other persons in the household that facilitates the labour force participation of persons with disabilities cannot be easily dismissed. Such assistance might involve transportation to and from work, help with dressing and personal appearance, and encouragement to pursue employment in the face of many barriers. The assistance may also go beyond needs that are related directly to the work. Persons with and without disabilities

---

20. One interpretation of these findings is that the support and assistance of other people in the home make it possible for persons with disabilities to work in the paid labour force. Those who live alone do not have access to such support or assistance as readily. However, another interpretation could be that some sort of selection process is involved, where, for whatever reason, persons least likely to be in the labour force are also less likely to be living with other people.

who are in the labour force often face competing demands on their time and energy. In order to arrive at a job prepared to work effectively, we must all perform some basic domestic tasks, such as shopping for food, preparing meals, cleaning or doing laundry. The demands on a person to both perform these tasks and work for pay often lead to a precarious balance. For persons with disabilities, the balance may be even more precarious. Depending upon the nature and severity of the disability, it may take more time and energy to perform these tasks, leaving little in reserve for paid work. Sharing domestic tasks with others may provide some persons with disabilities with more time and energy to pursue paid work.[21]

Table 2.3

Living arrangements for persons with disabilities by who performed domestic tasks, 1991

	Who performed domestic tasks			
	Self %	Self & others %	Someone else %	Total %
Meal preparation:				
Lived alone	89.2	6.3	4.5	100
Lived with others	43.8	28.4	27.8	100
Grocery shopping:				
Lived alone	80.2	15.4	4.4	100
Lived with others	33.9	36.0	30.0	100
Regular housework:				
Lived alone	85.2	7.6	7.2	100
Lived with others	37.8	31.9	30.3	100

See "Presentation of data" in Chapter 1 for assumption used.

21. It is also possible to get assistance from others and live alone. Relatives, neighbours, friends, volunteer workers and social service agencies can be a source of such assistance. However, the pool of potential helpers is greatly increased when someone else is living in the same household.

Among persons with disabilities, those who lived alone were much more likely to perform domestic tasks unaided by others than were those in shared living arrangements. For example, Table 2.3 demonstrates that 89.2 per cent of persons with disabilities who lived alone prepared their own meals, while only 43.8 per cent of those who lived with others did so. Similarly, 80.2 per cent of those who lived alone did their own grocery shopping, compared to only 33.9 per cent of those who lived with others. Finally, 85.2 per cent of those who lived alone did their own housework, but only 37.8 per cent of those who lived with others did. Living with others made it more likely that a person with a disability would be able to share domestic tasks. But did sharing domestic tasks make it easier for persons with disabilities to participate in the paid labour force?

It is impossible to know with certainty whether sharing domestic tasks made participating in the paid labour force easier. It certainly made it more likely. In general, the highest rates of labour force participation of persons with disabilities were among those who shared meal preparation, grocery shopping and housework with others, regardless of living arrangements. Those who performed these tasks by themselves as well as those who had these tasks performed entirely for them had the lowest rates of participation (Figure 2.12). For example, 62.4 per cent of persons who shared meal preparation with others were in the labour force, compared to 58.5 per cent of those who had someone else prepare their meals and only 52 per cent of those who prepared their own meals.

Certainly the sharing of domestic tasks seems to lead to greater labour force participation. But if some assistance with domestic tasks is good, should not having someone else perform these tasks entirely be even better? This depends on the reasons why individuals have varying degrees of assistance. Those who had someone else do domestic tasks entirely for them were more likely to have a severe disability and less likely to have a mild disability. Conversely, those who did these tasks by themselves were

most likely to have mild disabilities (Table 2.4). As we shall
see in the following section, labour force participation drops
as the severity of the disability increases. Thus, the lower
participation rates of those whose domestic tasks are
entirely performed by others is likely due to the more severe
nature of their disabilities.[22]

Figure 2.12

**Labour force participation rates* of persons with
disabilities by who performed specific domestic
tasks, 1991**

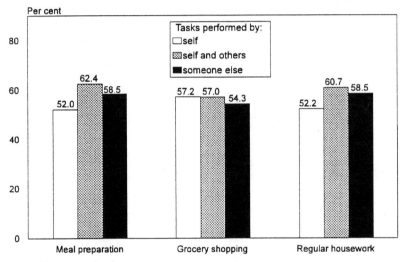

*employed or unemployed
See "Presentation of data" in Chapter 1 for assumptions used.

22. The data also show that persons with certain types of disabilities
    were more affected by such living arrangements than persons with
    other types of disabilities. For example, people with speaking,
    hearing or mental/learning disabilities seemed to benefit most, in
    terms of labour force participation, from shared living arrangements.
    However, it is interesting to note that persons with seeing disabilities
    were more likely to be in the labour force if they lived alone rather
    than with others.
        In addition, there were some rather significant sex differences in the
    relationship between living arrangements, who performs domestic
    tasks and labour force participation. These differences will be
    discussed in more detail in Chapter 6.

Table 2.4

Who performed specific domestic tasks among persons with disabilities, by severity of disability, 1991

	Severity			
	Mild %	**Moderate** %	**Severe** %	**Total** %
Meal preparation:				
Self	54.2	34.4	11.4	100
Self & others	55.2	29.1	15.7	100
Someone else	51.3	30.0	18.7	100
Grocery shopping:				
Self	60.6	31.1	8.3	100
Self & others	49.4	33.8	16.8	100
Someone else	48.9	31.0	20.1	100
Regular housework:				
Self	58.3	32.7	9.0	100
Self & others	52.4	34.3	13.3	100
Someone else	48.2	27.9	23.9	100

	Total number
Meal preparation:	
Self	1,065,000
Self & others	551,000
Someone else	580,000
Grocery shopping:	
Self	863,000
Self & others	718,000
Someone else	616,000
Regular housework:	
Self	949,000
Self & others	635,000
Someone else	609,000

See "Presentation of data" in Chapter 1 for assumptions used.

Factors affecting labour force participation: severity of disability

Labour force participation is also dependent upon the severity of one's disability. Severity of a disability is measured as a composite of two factors: the degree of loss of function involved with a particular disability, and the number of different disability types experienced. The greater the loss of function and the greater the number of disability types, the more severe the disability.[23]

As the severity of a person's disability increased, their likelihood of participating in the labour force decreased. In 1991, 70.9 per cent of persons with mild disabilities participated in the labour force, and while 44.8 per cent of those with moderate disabilities participated, only a quarter of those with severe disabilities were in the labour force (Figure 2.13). These figures represent an increase from 1986, with the greatest gains made by those with mild disabilities.

As illustrated in Figure 2.13, the labour force participation rate of persons with mild disabilities increased by nearly a fifth, from 59.4 per cent in 1986 to 70.9 per cent in 1991. The increased participation rate of those with moderate disabilities was considerably lower at 2.3 per cent (from 43.8 to 44.8 per cent). For those with severe disabilities, participation rates increased 14.8 per cent (from 22.3 to 25.6

23. In the HALS, degree of severity was measured by assigning points to individuals based on their answers to the screening questions. For example, an individual was assigned a single point if she or he reported having difficulty performing a particular task. Another point was assigned if the individual then said she or he was completely unable to perform the task. Thus, the total number of points assigned depended on the number of tasks an individual reported having difficulty performing as well as the degree of difficulty experienced (able to perform with some difficulty versus completely unable to perform). The range of all possible scores was divided into three intervals referred to as: mild (lowest scores), moderate and severe (highest scores). In 1991, 54.3 per cent of all persons aged 15 to 64 living in households had a mild disability; 31.6 per cent had a moderate disability; and 14.1 per cent had a severe disability.

per cent). However, the increase among those with severe disabilities appears to have been mostly a move from being identified as "out of the labour force" to being considered "unemployed," rather than to actual employment.

Table 2.5 shows that the greatest increase from 1986 to 1991 in the percentage identified as in the labour force but "unemployed" was among those with severe disabilities. The proportion of all working-age persons with severe disabilities who were unemployed increased by 50 per cent during that period (from 4.8 per cent to 7.2 per cent). The percentage of all working-age persons with severe disabilities who were employed increased by only 5.7 per cent, from 17.5 per cent to 18.5 per cent.[24]

Figure 2.13

Labour force participation rates* of persons with disabilities by severity level, 1986 and 1991

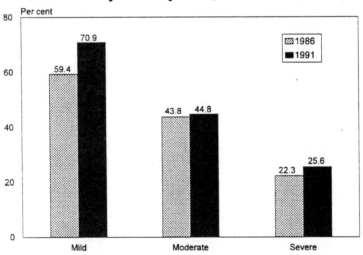

*employed or unemployed
See "Presentation of data" in Chapter 1 for assumptions used.

---

24. The meaning of the term "percentage unemployed" in Table 2.5 can be deceptive. These are not unemployment rates. As we shall see in the next chapter, the unemployment rate is calculated by taking the number of persons unemployed as a percentage of all those participating in the labour force (unemployed and employed). For some, however, the distinction between being unemployed and out of the labour force altogether may be somewhat blurred.

A certain proportion of those who are not in the labour force are individuals who have become so discouraged by constant unemployment that they have withdrawn from the labour market entirely. While these persons are technically considered to be out of the labour force, they are often referred to as the "hidden unemployed." The data in Table 2.5 indicate that, between 1986 and 1991, a higher proportion of persons with severe disabilities attempted to enter the labour force. Unfortunately, only a small proportion

Table 2.5

Labour force status of persons with disabilities by severity of disability, 1986 and 1991

		Labour force status				
Severity	Year	Employed %	Unemployed %	Part. rate %	Not in labour force %	Total %
Mild	1986	50.6	8.8	59.4	40.7	100
	1991	62.1	8.8	70.9	29.1	100
Moderate	1986	37.3	6.5	43.8	56.2	100
	1991	37.4	7.4	44.8	55.2	100
Severe	1986	17.5	4.8	22.3	77.7	100
	1991	18.5	7.2	25.6	74.4	100

Severity	Year	Total number
Mild	1986	890,000
	1991	1,249,000
Moderate	1986	573,000
	1991	725,000
Severe	1986	265,000
	1991	323,000

See "Presentation of data" in Chapter 1 for assumptions used.

had success in actually finding employment. Between 1986 and 1991, some of the "hidden unemployed" may have moved back into the labour market. The factors that caused such a shift are impossible to determine.

It is clear from Table 2.5 that persons with mild disabilities experienced the greatest increase in labour force participation and were more successful in finding jobs.

Factors affecting labour force participation: type of disability

The likelihood of participating in the paid labour force varied depending upon the nature of an individual's disability. In 1991, seven disability types were identified by the HALS:

- hearing
- seeing
- speaking
- agility
- mobility
- mental/learning
- unknown physical disabilities.[25]

The following section tracks the relationship between people's type of disability and their labour force participation. Additional variables – such as the number of disabilities, the severity of the disability and the requirements for special workplace accommodations – help us understand this relationship.

Disability type and labour force participation

As in 1986, those with unknown physical disabilities and hearing disabilities had the highest levels of labour force

---

25. Unknown physical disabilities are referred to in tables and graphs simply as "unknown" due to lack of space. Mental/learning disabilities are referred to as "mental" for the same reason.

participation in 1991. Those with speaking disabilities and mobility disabilities had the lowest rates of labour force participation (Figure 2.14).

Figure 2.14

Labour force participation rates* of persons with disabilities by disability type, 1991

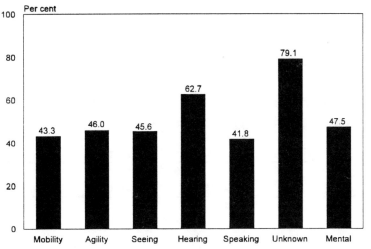

*employed or unemployed
See "Presentation of data" in Chapter 1 for assumptions used.

The label "unknown physical disability" is applied to persons who reported having a physical limitation, but did not report difficulty performing any of the specific tasks designed to capture mobility, agility, hearing, seeing, speaking or mental/learning disabilities. This is the only disability type listed that does not appear in combination with other types for any individual.

The participation rate among persons with an unknown physical disability was 79.1 per cent in 1991; this represented a 19.3 per cent increase since 1986, when the participation rate was 66.3 per cent (Table 2.6). Persons with hearing disabilities also had a relatively high rate of participation in the labour force at 62.7 per cent in 1991; this represented an increase of 16.1 per cent from 1986.

The greatest increase in labour force participation between 1986 and 1991 was among persons with seeing disabilities. In 1986, this group had the lowest rate of participation in the paid labour force at 35.1 per cent. With nearly a 30 per cent increase in participation, the rate for persons with seeing disabilities in 1991 was 45.6 per cent (Table 2.6).

Table 2.6

Labour force participation rates* for persons with disabilities by disability type**, 1986 and 1991

Disability type	Participation rates				
	1986 (%)	Rank***	1991 (%)	Rank***	% Increase
Mobility	40.8	4	43.3	6	6.1
Agility	41.8	3	46.0	4	10.0
Seeing	35.1	7	45.6	5	29.9
Hearing	54.0	2	62.7	2	16.1
Speaking	35.2	6	41.8	7	18.8
Unknown	66.3	1	79.1	1	19.3
Mental	38.0	5	47.5	3	25.0

Disability type	1991 Total number
Mobility	1,205,000
Agility	1,154,000
Seeing	212,000
Hearing	569,000
Speaking	179,000
Unknown	193,000
Mental	745,000

*employed or unemployed
**Note: Some individuals have more than one type of disability. The numbers in the final column, therefore, exceed the total number of persons with disabilities in Canada.
***Participation rate is ranked from highest (1) to lowest (7).
See "Presentation of data" in Chapter 1 for assumptions used.

The lowest increases in labour force participation were among persons with mobility and agility disabilities, which were the most prevalent of all types of disabilities.[26] Those with mobility disabilities increased their participation rate from 40.8 per cent in 1986 to 43.3 per cent in 1991, an increase of 6.1 per cent. For those with agility disabilities, the increase was 10 per cent (Table 2.6).

Disability type and number of disabilities

Many individuals report having more than one type of disability. In fact, certain disability types tend to cluster together; for example, people with agility disabilities often have mobility disabilities, and those with mental/learning disabilities frequently experience speaking disabilities.

As pointed out in *An Economic Profile of Persons with Disabilities in Canada*, multiple disabilities may create a greater employment disadvantage than single disabilities. Thus, the differences in labour force status by disability type could be partly due to the fact that some disabilities are either more or less likely to appear in combination than others.

> For example, a hearing disability may be no less disabling than any other single disability, but the very fact that it is found in isolation more often than any other disability may explain why it causes less employment disadvantage (assuming that multiple disabilities increase a person's employment disadvantage).[27]

In most instances, having multiple disabilities decreased labour force activity in 1991. The participation rates of

---

26. Some disability types are more prevalent than others. The following breakdown indicates the percentage of persons aged 15 to 64 with disabilities living in households, having each type of disability: mobility (52.5 per cent); agility (50.2 per cent); mental/learning (32.4 per cent); hearing (24.7 per cent); seeing (9.2 per cent); unknown physical (8.4 per cent); speaking (7.8 per cent).

27. Ross and Shillington, 1990, p. 50.

persons with only one disability were generally higher than those of persons with two disabilities[28] (summarized in Table 2.7).

Table 2.7

Labour force participation rates* by disability type** for those with one and two disabilities, 1991

	Only one disability		
Disability type	**Participation rate (%)**	**Rank*****	**Number**
Mobility	56.3	7	225,000
Agility	72.8	3	175,000
Seeing	61.9	5	45,000
Hearing	82.8	1	214,000
Speaking	65.8	4	19,000
Unknown	79.1	2	193,000
Mental	59.3	6	208,000

	Two disabilities		
Disability type	**Participation rate (%)**	**Rank*****	**Number**
Mobility	45.9	6	527,000
Agility	47.1	5	516,000
Seeing	68.5	3	44,000
Hearing	70.5	1	117,000
Speaking	69.2	2	40,000
Unknown	N/A	N/A	N/A
Mental	60.5	4	164,000

*employed or unemployed
**Note: Some individuals have more than one type of disability. The sum of the numbers in the final columns, therefore, exceed the total number of persons with disabilities in Canada.
***Participation rate is ranked from highest (1) to lowest (7).
N/A - no information available
See "Presentation of data" in Chapter 1 for assumptions used.

---

28. Although not shown here, the participation rate for persons with three or more disabilities is even lower than for those with two disabilities. Also, there is an exception among persons with seeing and speaking disabilities, as is evident in Table 2.7.

Even among persons with a single type of disability, labour force participation rates differed notably. People with hearing and unknown physical disabilities still had the highest rates of participation, at 82.8 per cent and 79.1 per cent respectively (Table 2.7). People with mobility and mental/learning disabilities still had comparatively low rates of participation. So, while certain multiple disabilities may have contributed to differences between people's labour force participation rates, by no means do they completely explain why some disability types seem to disadvantage some people more than others.

Disability type and severity

Is it possible that some of these differences in labour force participation rates by disability type occurred because some disabilities are more likely to be moderate or severe than others? Disability type by severity is summarized in Table 2.8. Persons with hearing and unknown physical disabilities have the highest rates of labour force participation. They are also the most likely to have a mild disability. In 1991, more than half of all those working-age adults with hearing disabilities were considered to have mild disabilities. Moreover, all of the unknown physical disabilities were mild. However, only about a quarter of persons with speaking disabilities, who had the lowest participation rate, were considered to have had mild disabilities. The persons with disabilities who had the lowest participation rates also had the lowest percentage of mild and the highest percentage of severe disabilities.

This is not surprising, given that people with more severe disabilities are less likely to be in the labour force. But does the variation in severity among disability types explain all of the differences in labour force participation?

If differences in severity explained all of the variation, we would see a similar rate of participation among people who had the same level of severity, regardless of their disability type. For example, all persons with mild disabilities would have similar rates of participation in the labour force, no

matter what their disability was. But this was not the case.
While the range in participation rates narrowed when
severity was "held constant" (as when comparing
participation rates by disability type within the same level of
severity), there was still a fair amount of variation in
participation rates across disability types.

When people with all severity levels were considered,
their participation rates ranged from a low of 41.8 per cent
for those with speaking disabilities to a high of 79.1 per cent
for those with unknown physical disabilities (Figure 2.14 on
page 49). However, when only those with mild disabilities
were considered, participation rates ranged from 60.4 per
cent for those with mobility disabilities to 79.6 per cent for
people with hearing disabilities (Figure 2.15). Among only
those with moderate disabilities, participation rates ranged
from 40.8 per cent for people with speaking disabilities to
54.2 per cent for those with hearing disabilities (Figure
2.16).[29] The range narrowed even more among persons
with severe disabilities; those with severe speaking
disabilities had the lowest rate of participation at 20.3 per

Table 2.8

Severity of disability by disability type*, 1991

Disability type	Mild %	Moderate %	Severe %	Total %	Total Number
Mobility	27.0	47.1	26.0	100	1,205,000
Agility	25.8	46.9	27.3	100	1,154,000
Seeing	34.2	34.1	31.7	100	212,000
Hearing	53.1	27.6	19.4	100	569,000
Speaking	24.9	43.3	31.8	100	179,000
Unknown	100.0	0.0	0.0	100	193,000
Mental	39.7	38.1	22.2	100	745,000

*Note: Some individuals have more than one type of disability. The
   sum of the numbers in the final column, therefore, exceeds the total
   number of persons with disabilities in Canada.
See "Presentation of data" in Chapter 1 for assumptions used.

29. There were no working-age persons with moderate or severe
     unknown physical disabilities.

Figure 2.15

Labour force participation rates* of persons with disabilities by disability type for those with <u>mild disabilities</u>, 1991

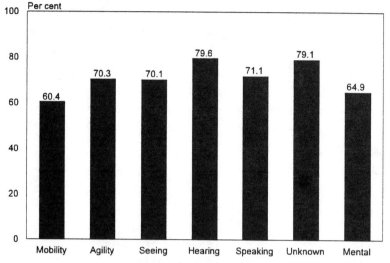

*employed or unemployed
See "Presentation of data" in Chapter 1 for assumptions used.

Figure 2.16

Labour force participation rates* of persons with disabilities by disability type for those with <u>moderate disabilities</u>, 1991

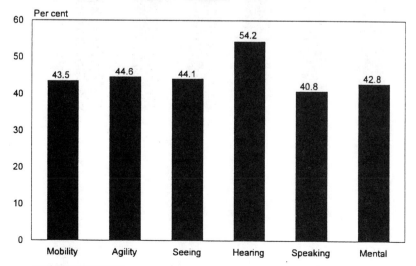

*employed or unemployed
See "Presentation of data" in Chapter 1 for assumptions used.

cent, and those with severe hearing disabilities had the highest rate of participation at 28.4 per cent (Figure 2.17).

While severity is certainly an important factor in explaining variations in participation rates by disability type, it does not explain all of the differences. Within each level of severity in 1991, hearing or unknown disabilities continued to be associated with the highest levels of labour force participation. Similarly, people with speaking, mental/learning, mobility and seeing disabilities tended to have the lowest rates of participation, even when the level of severity was held constant.

Figure 2.17

Labour force participation rates* of persons with disabilities by disability type for those with <u>severe disabilities</u>, 1991

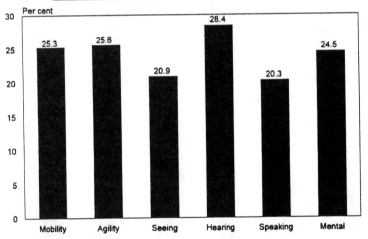

*employed or unemployed
See "Presentation of data" in Chapter 1 for assumptions used.

Disability type and workplace accommodations

Another factor that might contribute to the variation in participation rates among people with different types of disabilities is their requirement for special workplace accommodations. People with some disability types are less likely than others to require certain workplace accommodations (Table 2.9).[30] For example, in 1991, persons with unknown physical and hearing disabilities were the least likely to require accessible transportation to get to and from work; they were also the least likely to need their job redesigned or their working hours or days modified. Not surprisingly, they also had the highest labour force participation rates.

There is no doubt that people requiring particular workplace accommodations were less likely to participate in

Table 2.9

Percentage of persons with disabilities requiring selected workplace accommodations, by disability type*, 1991

Disability type	Accessible transportation %	Job redesign %	Modified hrs/days %	Total number
Mobility	11.6	26.1	30.1	1,050,000
Agility	12.2	27.9	30.3	1,005,000
Seeing	16.4	27.6	29.4	181,000
Hearing	7.6	16.3	17.8	463,000
Speaking	20.8	34.7	33.4	152,000
Unknown	3.7	13.1	13.1	169,000
Mental	13.5	26.1	29.2	651,000

*Note: Some individuals have more than one type of disability. The sum of the numbers in the final column, therefore, exceeds the total number of persons with disabilities in Canada.
See "Presentation of data" in Chapter 1 for assumptions used.

30. Information on requirements for workplace accommodations is not available for self-employed persons or unpaid workers in family businesses. Table 2.9 and Figures 2.18 and 2.19 apply to all those persons aged 15 to 64 with disabilities (employed, unemployed and out of the labour force) who were *not* self-employed or unpaid workers in a family business.

the labour force (Figure 2.18). Among those who required accessible transportation to and from work, only 25.2 per cent were in the labour force; among those who did not require such transportation, 55.9 per cent were either employed or seeking work. Similarly, among those who required job redesign, 36.1 per cent participated in the labour force, compared to 57.5 per cent of those who did not have such a requirement. Finally, among those who required modified work hours or days, only 28.6 per cent participated in the labour force. The participation rate of those without such a requirement was more than double this figure at 60.1 per cent (Figure 2.18)

Having a requirement for special work accommodations certainly reduced labour force participation. However, only a minority of working-age persons with disabilities actually reported such requirements. Thus, the overall impact of such requirements on the relationship between disability type and participation rate is likely to have been small. One useful way of demonstrating this is to examine the

Figure 2.18

Labour force participation rates* of persons with disabilities by requirement for special accommodations, 1991

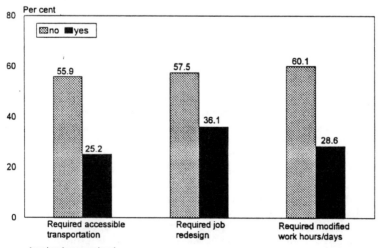

*employed or unemployed
See "Presentation of data" in Chapter 1 for assumptions used.

participation rates by disability type of those persons with disabilities who did not report any of the three requirements mentioned. Figure 2.19 indicates that when those requiring accessible transportation, job redesign or modified work schedules were eliminated from the analysis, the range of participation rates among disability types narrowed only slightly. The dominant pattern detected earlier in Figure 2.14 is still quite evident in Figure 2.19; that is, those with unknown physical and hearing disabilities had much higher rates of participation.

According to the 1991 HALS, people with some disability types faced more barriers in entering the labour force than did those with other disability types. Some of these barriers took the form of requirements for accessible transportation, modified work hours or days, and job redesign, among

Figure 2.19

Labour force participation rates* of persons with disabilities not requiring special transportation, modified work hours or job redesign, by disability type, 1991

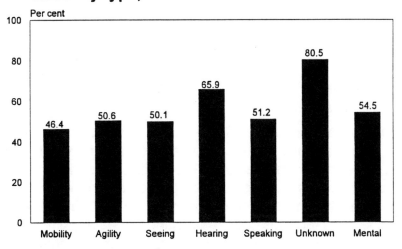

*employed or unemployed
See "Presentation of data" in Chapter 1 for assumptions used.

others. Many other barriers cannot be adequately measured in the survey data available. In particular, the attitudes of employers toward certain disabilities may play a large part in the differences in labour force activity of people with different types of disabilities.

Factors affecting labour force participation: cause of disability

The underlying cause of a person's disability also appears to affect their participation in the labour force. People with disabilities which had a work-related cause (injuries or industrial diseases) had the highest participation rates (65 per cent). People with disabilities which had multiple causes experienced the lowest participation rates (41 per cent). Ranked from highest participation rate to lowest, the underlying causes of disabilities identified in the 1991 HALS were:

- work-related causes
- undetermined causes
- non-work accidents
- causes that existed at birth
- aging
- diseases or illnesses
- multiple causes (See Figure 2.20)

The underlying cause of a disability is also linked to its severity. Disabilities with multiple causes were the most likely to be moderate or severe. Disabilities caused by disease or illness and those which existed at birth were also more likely than most to be moderate or severe. On the other hand, disabilities caused by aging or undetermined factors were the most likely to be mild. The proportion of disabilities which were either moderate or severe by underlying cause was as follows:

- multiple causes (78 per cent either moderate or severe)
- diseases or illnesses (54 per cent)
- causes that existed at birth (53 per cent)
- non-work accidents (51 per cent)
- work-related causes (45 per cent)
- undetermined causes (34 per cent)
- aging (32 per cent) (See Figure 2.21)

Given these findings, and the fact that labour force participation rates decreased as severity increased, it is not surprising that disabilities with multiple causes (being more

Figure 2.20

Labour force participation rates* of persons with disabilities by cause of disability, 1991

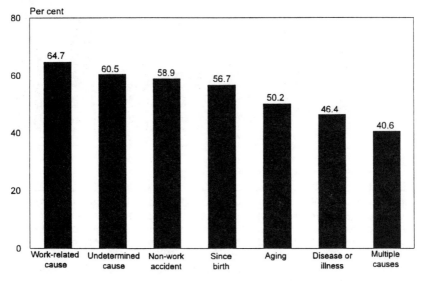

*employed or unemployed
See "Presentation of data" in Chapter 1 for assumptions used.

severe overall) would be associated with lower participation rates. Similarly, it is also understandable that disabilities which were either work-related or caused by undetermined factors (being less severe overall) would be associated with higher participation rates. However, persons with disabilities caused by aging, who tended to have the mildest disabilities overall, also had a fairly low participation rate in 1991. The lack of participation in the labour market by individuals who reported aging as the underlying cause of their disability may simply reflect their decision to take early retirement.[31]

Figure 2.21

Proportion of persons with either moderate or severe disabilities by cause of disability, 1991

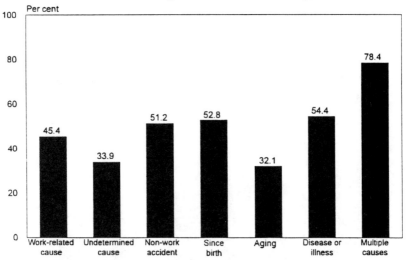

See "Presentation of data" in Chapter 1 for assumptions used.

31. For older men, in particular, this is likely to reflect early retirement. For older women, however, it may reflect differences in societal expectations. Older women would have entered their adult years at a time when their traditional role was defined primarily as a homemaker performing unpaid work. The dramatic rise in the participation of women in the labour force since the 1960s reflects the changing definition of women's roles in society. However, we do not yet know what younger women in the labour force will do as they age. While they may have higher rates of participation when they reach age 55 to 64 than today's older women, it is also possible that they will follow the trend set by men toward early retirement. As well, any number of social, economic and legislative factors may alter the degree of labour force activity among persons in this older age group in the future.

Differences in the severity levels of people's disabilities do not explain all of the variation in their labour force participation rates. Even when we examine only individuals with disabilities of the same severity level, some variation remains in their rates of labour force participation. For example, considering only persons with mild disabilities (Figure 2.22), those with disabilities due to work-related causes had noticeably higher rates of participation (81.1 per cent) than those with disabilities due to illness and disease (63.6 per cent). Those with disabilities due to most of the other causes had participation rates clustered closely together in the 70 to 73 per cent range. This suggests that severity level was a key factor in explaining the variation in participation rates among these disabilities.

Clearly, persons with disabilities due to work-related causes were more likely to be in the labour force and those with disabilities due to illness/disease were less likely to participate. Most of the variation in labour force participation

Figure 2.22

Labour force participation rates* of persons with mild disabilities by cause of disability, 1991

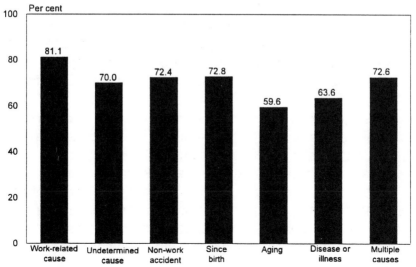

*employed or unemployed
See "Presentation of data" in Chapter 1 for assumptions used.

rates for those with disabilities due to other causes was the result of differences in either severity or age. It may be that there were more accommodations, services, and special programs in place for persons who acquired their disability due to work-related causes. This could be due to public and private insurance programs that provide financial assistance and rehabilitation or retraining programs to encourage individuals to return to work. At the same time, employers may feel a greater obligation to help an individual return to work if that person acquired a disability as a result of an accident or from exposure to hazardous substances on the job.[32]

Persons with disabilities caused by illness and disease may be more restricted in their eligibility for various insurance or income-support programs, compared to those with disabilities due to work-related causes. As well, employers may be less inclined to make special accommodations for such individuals and may be more likely to fear a worsening of the individual's condition as the illness or disease progresses.

Discussion

As will be seen in Chapter 5, persons with disabilities who had earnings from employment were much less likely to live in poverty than those who did not. The first step in securing such earnings, however, is to enter the labour force.

Entering and staying in the labour force can be a major hurdle for some people with disabilities. The path is often littered with obstacles and closed doors. Whether or not persons with disabilities believe they are limited or prevented from working depends upon their environment as much as it does upon their disability. As seen in Chapter 1, it is the interaction between one's disability and one's environment that produces a handicap. This chapter has

---

32. It is also possible that those with work-related disabilities may simply have a greater attachment to the paid labour force.

reviewed a number of factors that affect the likelihood of labour force participation for persons with disabilities.[33] As well, it has reviewed some of the changes in labour force participation that took place between 1986 and 1991.

Within those five years, the labour force participation rate for persons with disabilities increased from 48.5 per cent to 56.3 per cent. More than a third of this increase was likely due to the overall higher levels of education attained by working-age persons with disabilities during the same period. Education was instrumental in the labour force participation of persons with disabilities. For example, in 1991, the participation rate of persons with disabilities who had a university degree was nearly double that of those with primary school or lower (73 per cent compared to about 38 per cent).

Persons who had their disability before they completed their education tended to attain higher levels of education than those who acquired their disability after completing school; this was true regardless of age. This indicates that those who know they will have a disability in the future can take steps to mitigate some of the difficulties they will face in the labour force.

Besides being more likely to invest in higher education, those who had their disability before completing school also had higher labour force participation rates than those who acquired their disability after completing school – even if they had attained the same level of education. This effect was especially pronounced among those with a university degree. Again, it may be possible that the ability to plan one's education around a disability (both in terms of the amount and type of education) enhances the likelihood of being in the labour force.

---

33. There are more environmental factors that affect participation in the paid labour force among persons with disabilities than those investigated here, but the HALS does not allow an analysis of all such factors.

Higher education may be one of the best ways for
persons with disabilities to improve their labour market
opportunities. Greater flexibility in the school system during
recent years for those with disabilities may also have helped
younger people with disabilities to achieve higher levels of
education. This may have contributed to the overall increase
in educational attainment among working-age people with
disabilities between 1986 and 1991. For example, among
those who had their disability before completing school,
younger people were more likely to have had the opportunity
to attend special classes or take a lighter load of courses or
correspondence courses. Among those who had the
disability before completing school, 37.5 per cent of those
aged 15 to 24 were able to attend special classes at some
point during their education, while only 5.9 per cent of their
counterparts aged 45 to 64 had such an opportunity.

Such accommodations at the school level could have
helped students with disabilities to complete their education.
This does not mean, however, that students with disabilities
now have all the accommodations they require in the school
system. As noted by Jennifer Leigh Hill:

> Students with disabilities face a number of
> unique barriers that may prevent them from
> pursuing a program of higher education...
> Without consideration of their unique learning
> needs, many students with disabilities may be
> doomed to fail, even before they put their foot
> inside the door that may offer them the
> opportunities to be successful and to achieve
> in the competitive world that faces them in the
> future.[34]

For those who are able to do so, obtaining a higher
education may be their best strategy for mitigating the
negative effects of their disability. For those who acquire a
disability after their education has been completed, higher
education may lessen some of the hardships they face when

---

34. Hill, 1996, p. 125.

attempting to enter or stay in the labour force. Nevertheless, in 1991, persons with disabilities at every educational level had lower levels of labour force participation than did others. So, education for persons with disabilities is not the only solution to breaking down labour force barriers.

As mentioned earlier, environmental factors determine whether or not a disability reaches the level of handicap. One factor that was proven to affect the labour force participation of those with a disability was whether the individual lived alone or with others. In 1991, persons with disabilities who lived with others were more likely to participate in the paid labour force than those who lived alone. This is the opposite of the trend among persons without disabilities.

By living with others, persons with disabilities may be able to obtain the assistance they need in order to participate in the labour force. This assistance may include transportation to and from work, help with dressing and personal hygiene, or the reading of work-related materials (if one has a seeing disability, for example). Other household members may also provide emotional support and encouragement. The available data do not allow us to assess the importance of such encouragement. But, more than five per cent of persons with disabilities who were not in the labour force reported that the "discouragement" of family members and friends was a major barrier to their entering the labour force. If discouragement is a barrier, encouragement is likely to be a facilitator.

In addition, other persons in the household are able to help out with everyday domestic chores, such as shopping, meal preparation and housework. For some persons with disabilities, such tasks may take longer to perform and require more energy. This can affect the amount of time and energy available for sleeping, eating and working for pay. Persons with disabilities who lived with others in 1991 were much more likely to share such domestic tasks than those who lived alone, and those who shared such domestic tasks with others were more likely to participate in the paid labour force.

Certain characteristics surrounding a person's disability also seemed to influence their participation in the paid labour force. The severity, type and cause of the disability were investigated in this chapter. A great deal of variation in participation rates occurred across levels of severity. The rate of labour force participation ranged from 25.6 per cent among persons with severe disabilities to 70.9 per cent among persons with mild disabilities.

While people with all severity levels of disabilities participated in the labour force in 1991 in greater numbers than compared to 1986, the largest increases occurred among those with mild disabilities. People in this group increased their participation rate by 19.4 per cent between 1986 and 1991. Those with severe disabilities experienced a 14.8 per cent increase during the same period. Furthermore, among those with severe disabilities, the move into the labour market seems to have been more often a move into unemployment. It is possible that some of the "hidden unemployed" merely became officially unemployed. Whatever factors may have encouraged persons with disabilities to participate in the labour market in increasing numbers, it appears that those with mild disabilities met with greater success. While these increases are encouraging and an indication of the work potential of persons with disabilities, the gap between those with mild and those with severe disabilities grew wider.

People with certain disability types also had higher participation rates than others. For example, persons with unknown physical and hearing disabilities were much more likely to be in the labour force than those with other types of disabilities. These two types of disabilities, however, were also less likely to require workplace accommodations and were more likely to be mild than other types. However, even when the severity level was held constant, those with unknown physical and hearing disabilities were still more likely to participate in the labour force in greater numbers. It may be that hearing and unknown physical disabilities interact with environmental factors in a manner that is less likely to create a handicap. These environmental factors may include building design, the configuration and proportions of work stations and office equipment, and other features of the physical environment which may be less accessible or user-friendly to people with some disability types compared to others. Differences in attitudes on the part of employers toward people with various types of disabilities may also be a factor.

In the 1991 data, the underlying cause of a person's disability also seemed to influence their participation rate. Some underlying causes were associated with more severe disabilities than others, and the more severe the disability, the less the likelihood of participating in the labour force. However, regardless of the severity level, persons with disabilities due to work-related causes were more likely to participate in the labour force and those with disabilities caused by illness or disease were less likely to do so. There may have been more programs in place, and a greater willingness on the part of employers to reintegrate those persons who acquired a disability directly as a result of their work. Persons with disabilities caused by illness or disease may have faced a very different set of opportunities and attitudes.

Age and sex (and the interaction between the two) were also highly linked to labour force participation for persons with disabilities. Older people were less likely to be in the labour force. While this reflects the trend toward early retirement found in the general population, it was more pronounced among persons with disabilities. As in the general population, women with disabilities participated less than their male counterparts. However, this gap narrowed among persons with disabilities between 1986 and 1991, as women with disabilities increased their participation rate at a much faster pace than men. The analysis of sex differences in labour force participation will be expanded upon in Chapter 6.

Getting into the labour force is the first hurdle on the road to greater economic security for persons with disabilities. For those who are in the labour force, there are additional hurdles. The following chapter is devoted to an investigation of persons with disabilities in the labour force – their successes and their challenges.

Chapter 3

In the labour force:
Successes and challenges

The previous chapter discussed the gaps in labour force participation *between* people with and without disabilities, as well as *among* those with disabilities. This chapter deals with the experiences of persons with disabilities who were in the labour force in 1991. A common theme emerges from both chapters.

The greatest labour force challenge for persons with disabilities appears to be getting a job. Once employment has been secured, the differences between those with and without disabilities are less pronounced, though still problematic. In order to get a job, one faces two hurdles: first, one must enter the labour force, and second, one must then find employment. Persons with disabilities are at a disadvantage at both of these stages. As discussed in the previous chapter, the 1991 HALS data show that persons with disabilities were less likely to enter the labour force. And, as this chapter will explain, once in the labour force, they were less likely to find a job.

Persons with disabilities who were employed continued to face challenges in the labour market.[1] In many ways, however, the experiences of employed persons with disabilities were not as dissimilar from those of persons without disabilities as one might expect. Contrary to what some may believe, the vast majority of persons with disabilities who worked in the labour force did so on a full-time basis. As revealed later in this chapter, persons with disabilities were only slightly less likely to work full-time hours than those without disabilities. Also, given the labour force disadvantages faced by persons with disabilities already discussed, one might expect a large gap in earnings between employed persons with and without disabilities. But, while there was an earnings disadvantage for persons with disabilities, it was not as great as one might expect. The similarities between the distribution of earnings of persons with and without disabilities are also examined in this chapter.

While many people with disabilities were quite successful in the labour market, certain groups faced difficulties at each and every step of the way. Among those most negatively affected were persons with severe disabilities, women with disabilities and persons with mental/learning or speaking disabilities. These individuals faced a great disadvantage even when they did find jobs – most obviously evident in their substantially lower earnings.

As the previous chapter showed, higher education was one factor that appeared to provide a decided advantage in the labour force to persons with disabilities. This chapter continues to highlight the benefits of education for persons with disabilities by demonstrating its value in obtaining a job and increasing one's earning potential.

---

1.   For example, one-third of employed persons with disabilities said
      they believed their disability would make it difficult for them to
      change jobs or advance in their present job.

Finding a job

Persons with disabilities who were in the labour force were less successful in finding a job than persons without disabilities. In 1991, 14.4 per cent of those aged 15 to 64 with disabilities in the labour force were unemployed, compared to 9.8 per cent of those without disabilities (Figure 3.1).[2]

Sex and unemployment

The unemployment rate for women and men without disabilities was similar in 1991, at 9.9 per cent and 9.7 per cent respectively. However, among persons with disabilities there were some notable sex differences. Women with disabilities who were in the labour force were more likely to encounter problems finding employment than their male counterparts. For men with disabilities, the unemployment

Figure 3.1

Unemployment rates* of women and men with and without disabilities, 1991

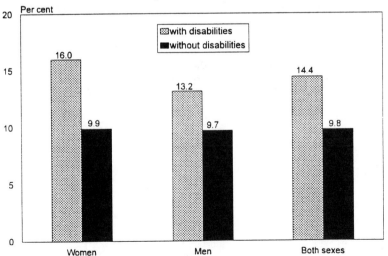

*proportion of persons in the labour force who were unemployed
See "Presentation of data" in Chapter 1 for assumptions used.

2. The unemployment rate in 1991 was down slightly from 1986 for persons with and without disabilities. In 1986, the unemployment rate for persons with disabilities was 15.3 per cent and for persons without disabilities, 10.3 per cent.

rate was 13.2 per cent; for women with disabilities, it was 16 per cent (Figure 3.1).

Age and unemployment

Young people in the labour force, both with and without disabilities, faced unusually high unemployment in 1991. Among those aged 15 to 24 with disabilities, the unemployment rate was 20.1 per cent; for the same age group without disabilities, the figure was 15.3 per cent (Figure 3.2). Among those aged 25 to 44, unemployment rates were considerably lower at 14.7 per cent for persons with disabilities and 8.8 per cent for persons without disabilities. Among those aged 45 to 64, 12.2 per cent of those with disabilities and 7.8 per cent of those without disabilities in the labour force were unemployed.

Severity of the disability and unemployment

People with severe disabilities have startlingly high rates of unemployment. As noted in the previous chapter, they had much lower rates of labour force participation than those with mild disabilities, and that gap increased between

Figure 3.2

Unemployment rates* of persons with and without disabilities by age group, 1991

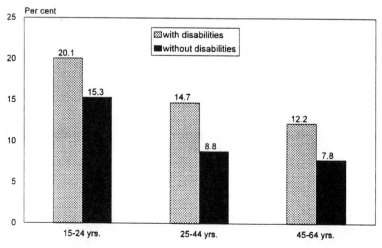

*proportion of persons in the labour force who were unemployed
See "Presentation of data" in Chapter 1 for assumptions used.

1986 and 1991. It is not difficult to imagine how discouraged someone with a severe disability might feel when facing an unemployment rate of 27.9 per cent (Figure 3.3). Such discouragement could, understandably, result in an individual dropping out of the labour force altogether. This, in part, might help to explain the lower rates of labour force participation of persons with severe disabilities.

While the unemployment rate of persons with mild disabilities dropped by 16 per cent between 1986 and 1991 (to 12.4 per cent), the unemployment rate of those with moderate and severe disabilities increased during the same period. The unemployment rate for persons with moderate disabilities increased by 11 per cent (to 16.5 per cent). For those with severe disabilities, it jumped by 30 per cent (to 27.9 per cent). It would appear that the years between 1986 and 1991 were much kinder to persons with mild disabilities than to those with more severe disabilities.

Figure 3.3

Unemployment rates* of persons with disabilities by severity of disability, 1986 and 1991

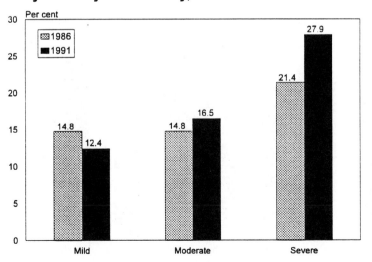

*proportion of persons in the labour force who were unemployed
See "Presentation of data" in Chapter 1 for assumptions used.

Disability type and unemployment

As revealed in the previous chapter, persons with hearing and unknown physical disabilities had the highest rates of participation in the labour force. It is not surprising, therefore, that persons with either of these two disability types, once they were in the labour force, also had the lowest rates of unemployment. Persons with hearing disabilities had an unemployment rate of 10.4 per cent in 1991, only slightly higher than the 9.8 per cent unemployment rate of persons without disabilities . For those with unknown physical disabilities, the unemployment rate in 1991 was 13.3 per cent, and the rate for those with seeing disabilities was not far behind at 13.5 per cent (Figure 3.4).

Even though they had the third highest labour force participation rate among the seven disability types listed, persons with mental/learning disabilities had the highest rate

Figure 3.4

Unemployment rates* of persons with disabilities by disability type, 1991

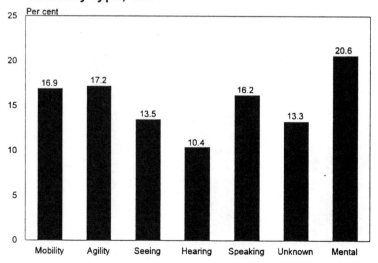

*proportion of persons in the labour force who were unemployed
See "Presentation of data" in Chapter 1 for assumptions used.

of unemployment.[3] Nearly 21 per cent of those with mental/learning disabilities who were in the labour force were unable to find employment. Between 16.2 and 17.2 per cent of those with speaking, mobility or agility disabilities in the labour force were unemployed.

Cause of the disability and unemployment

As was noted previously, people with disabilities resulting from either multiple causes or aging had low rates of labour force participation. Those with disabilities arising from multiple causes were less likely to participate in the labour force mainly because of the severity of their disabilities. The low participation rates of those with disabilities caused by aging (most of which were mild) were likely due to their decision to take early retirement.

Persons in the labour force who had disabilities caused by aging, however, had a relatively low rate of unemployment at 11.1 per cent (Figure 3.5). The next lowest

Figure 3.5

Unemployment rates* of persons with disabilities by cause of disability, 1991

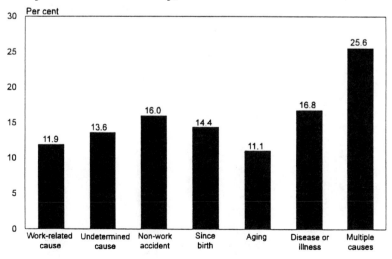

*proportion of persons in the labour force who were unemployed
See "Presentation of data" in Chapter 1 for assumptions used.

3. This suggests that this group was certainly interested in paid employment, but encountered considerable difficulty in obtaining it.

rate of unemployment was among people whose disabilities were caused by work-related factors (11.9 per cent). This group also had a fairly high rate of labour force participation. Persons with disabilities due to multiple causes had the highest rate of unemployment at 25.6 per cent.

Though not illustrated, further analysis reveals that people with disabilities stemming from multiple causes tended to have the highest levels of unemployment regardless of the severity of their disability. So while the low participation rate of the people in this group can be explained almost entirely by differences in the severity of their disabilities, their high unemployment rate cannot.

Education and unemployment

The labour force advantage provided by higher levels of education was reflected in unemployment rates as starkly as it was in participation rates in the previous chapter (Figure 3.6). In 1991, the completion of post-secondary schooling resulted in the lowest rates of unemployment for persons

Figure 3.6

Unemployment rates* of persons with and without disabilities by highest level of education, 1991

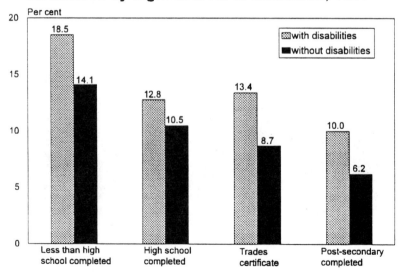

*proportion of persons in the labour force who were unemployed
See "Presentation of data" in Chapter 1 for assumptions used.

with disabilities (10 per cent unemployed) and for those without disabilities (6.2 per cent unemployed). By comparison, persons with disabilities who had not completed high school had an unemployment rate of 18.5 per cent, and those without disabilities with the same level of education had an unemployment rate of 14.1 per cent.

While education certainly reduced the likelihood that a person would be unemployed, it did not create a "level playing field" between persons with and without disabilities. At each level of education, persons with disabilities had higher rates of unemployment than those without disabilities. In fact, the 10 per cent unemployment rate of persons with disabilities who had post-secondary education was very close to the unemployment rate of persons without disabilities whose highest educational credential was a high school diploma (10.5 per cent).

Occupation and unemployment

Unemployment rates varied by occupation both for persons with disabilities and for those without (Figure 3.7).

Figure 3.7

Unemployment rates* of persons with and without disabilities by occupational group, 1991

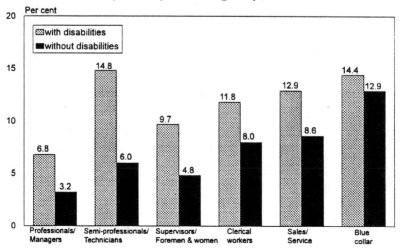

*proportion of persons in the labour force who were unemployed
See "Presentation of data" in Chapter 1 for assumptions used.

People in professional or upper-level managerial occupations had the lowest unemployment rates of all groups in 1991. Those with disabilities who worked or sought work in professional or managerial occupations had an unemployment rate of 6.8 per cent. Those without disabilities in these occupations had an unemployment rate of only 3.2 per cent. However, both persons with and without disabilities in blue-collar occupations had high rates of unemployment: for those with disabilities, the rate was 14.4 per cent; for those without disabilities, it was 12.9 per cent.[4]

The difference in the unemployment rates of people with and without disabilities was noticeably less among the three occupational groups on the right in Figure 3.7 (clerical workers, sales/service workers and blue-collar workers) and greater for the three occupational groups on the left in the figure (professionals/managers, semi-professionals/ technicians and supervisors/foremen/forewomen).

Nevertheless, people with disabilities experienced consistently higher unemployment across all occupational groups. Having a disability appeared to constitute an employment "penalty" that was much larger for some occupations than others. People with disabilities seemed to face the greatest barriers when trying to gain employment as managers, professionals, semi-professionals or technicians.

The greatest difference in the unemployment rates of people with and without disabilities was among semi-professionals and technicians. The unemployment rate of persons without disabilities working or seeking work as semi-professionals or technicians was only 6 per cent. However, the unemployment rate of persons with disabilities in the same occupational group was more than double at 14.8 per cent.

---

4.   This might have been due to the economic restructuring during this time.

It appears that rates of unemployment among persons with disabilities who were semi-professionals or technicians varied greatly depending upon their sex. A breakdown of unemployment rates by occupational group and sex reveals that men with disabilities who were semi-professionals or technicians did not face unusually high unemployment. But their female counterparts did. Therefore, high unemployment rates among these groups appeared to be a problem primarily for women with disabilities (not illustrated).

Requirements for special accommodations and unemployment

Whether or not people with disabilities required special accommodations in order to work also had an impact on their employment prospects. The three types of special accommodations considered here are: accessible transportation, job redesign and modified schedules (such as shorter work days or weeks). In each case, the unemployment rate of persons requiring such accommodations was nearly double that of those who did not. For example, in 1991, 14.8 per cent of persons in the

Figure 3.8

Unemployment rates* of persons with disabilities by requirement for special accommodations, 1991

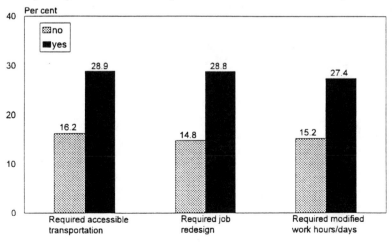

* proportion of persons in the labour force who were unemployed
See "Presentation of data" in Chapter 1 for assumptions used.

labour force who did not need their job redesigned were
unemployed, compared to 28.8 per cent of those who had
such a requirement[5] (Figure 3.8). It would appear that
finding employment was a much greater challenge for
people with special needs.

From the data presented thus far, it appears that persons
with disabilities in 1991 found it much more difficult to get a
job than those without disabilities. Women, persons with
severe disabilities, those with mental/learning disabilities,
those with lower levels of education, and those with a
requirement for special accommodations had the greatest
difficulty. But did those people with disabilties who found
paid employment work the same amount of time and have
similar earnings as persons without disabilities?

Full-time/part-time work patterns

Some may believe that persons with disabilities are
much more likely than others to work part-time. Thus, one
might expect to see a huge gap in the rates of full-time
employment of persons with and without disabilities. In fact,
in 1991 that gap was very small. Of those persons without
disabilities who reported working at least one hour a week,
82.9 per cent were working full-time or 30 hours per week or
more. Only a slightly lower percentage of persons with
disabilities (80.9 per cent) were working similar hours
(Figure 3.9). A number of factors appeared to affect the
participation of people with disabilities in full-time work.

Just under a third of persons with disabilities who were
unemployed in 1991 were seeking part-time employment;
half wanted full-time employment and the remaining fifth
were willing to take either full-time or part-time work. Just
over half of those who were seeking part-time employment
made that choice because of their disability. This means that
disability itself forced only 16 per cent of all unemployed

---

5.   This excludes individuals in the labour force who were self-
     employed or working without pay in a family business.

persons with disabilities to seek part-time employment.[6] Clearly, the majority of people with disabilities in the labour force either had or wanted full-time work.

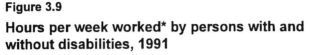

Figure 3.9

Hours per week worked* by persons with and without disabilities, 1991

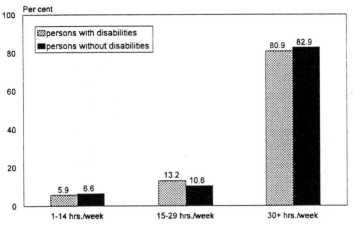

*includes persons in the labour force who reported working at least one hour a week
See "Presentation of data" in Chapter 1 for assumptions used.

The number of hours worked per week by women and men

As noted in the previous chapter, women with and without disabilities were less likely than men to participate in the labour force. It is not surprising, therefore, that women were also less likely to work full-time when employed. However, this relationship between sex and full-time employment was not unique to persons with disabilities. The rate of full-time employment among women was roughly 80 per cent of that for men, for both those with and without disabilities. As illustrated in Figure 3.10, 70.9 per cent of employed women with disabilities and 88.3 per cent of employed men with disabilities worked full-time in 1991; similarly, 73.6 per cent of employed women without

6.   If 55 per cent of those seeking only part-time work were doing so because of their disability, and about 29 per cent of those unemployed looking for work were seeking only part-time work, then 16 per cent (.55 x .29) of all those with disabilities who were unemployed were seeking only part-time work due to their disability.

disabilities and 90.4 per cent of employed men without
disabilities worked full-time in the same year.[7]

Figure 3.10

Percentage of women and men with and without disabilities who worked 30 hours per week* or more, 1991

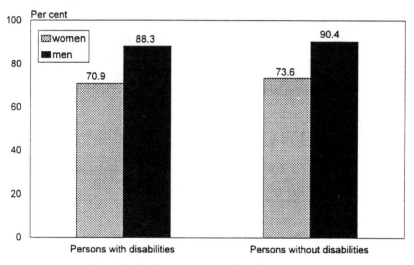

*includes persons in the labour force who reported working at least one hour a week
See "Presentation of data" in Chapter 1 for assumptions used.

Living arrangements and the number of hours worked per week

Shared living arrangements appeared to facilitate entry
into the labour force for persons with disabilities.[8] Therefore,
one might expect that living with others would also facilitate
full-time employment for persons with disabilities. Men with
disabilities in shared living arrangements were more likely to

---

7.   Among both women and men with disabilities, those between 25
      and 44 years of age were the most likely to work full-time. In 1991,
      about 93 per cent of men and 74 per cent of women with disabilities
      in this age group worked full-time. The rate of full-time employment
      was slightly lower among women and men in the next oldest age
      group (45 to 64). Those aged 15 to 24 were the least likely to report
      working full-time hours, because of the many students in this age
      group who chose to work part-time while attending school.

8.   This was not the case for those without disabilities.

be employed full-time than those who lived alone.[9]
However, this was not true for women (see Figure 3.11).
Among employed women with disabilities who lived alone in
1991, 74.6 per cent worked full-time (30 hours per week or
more); among those who lived with others, 70.7 per cent
worked full-time. However, among employed men with
disabilities who lived alone, 82.3 per cent worked full-time,
compared to 89.3 per cent of those who lived with others. It
is interesting to note that among both women with and
without disabilities, living with others increased their
likelihood of working part-time. This is, no doubt, due to
domestic responsibilities (primarily childrearing).

Figure 3.11

**Percentage of women and men with and without
disabilities who worked 30 hours per week*
or more, by living arrangements, 1991**

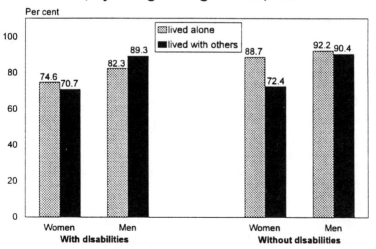

*includes persons in the labour force who reported working at least one hour a week
See "Presentation of data" in Chapter 1 for assumptions used.

---

9. This was not true for men without disabilities, who were more likely
    to work full-time if they lived alone.

Severity of the disability and the number of hours worked per week

Another factor that had an impact on the likelihood of a person with a disability working full-time was the severity of the disability. Persons with mild disabilities were more likely to work full-time than those with severe disabilities (Figure 3.12). In 1991, 83 per cent of employed persons with mild disabilities worked full-time (30 hours or more per week), compared to 72.3 per cent of those with severe disabilities.

There are at least two plausible explanations for this. The first is that persons with severe disabilities may be more likely to choose part-time employment because of their condition and environmental factors. However, from the 1991 HALS data, it is difficult to determine the degree to which employed persons with severe disabilities chose to work full-time or part-time. Reporting a need for a modified work schedule might be one indicator of the likelihood of choosing part-time work because of one's disability. Nearly 40 per cent of all those in the labour force (employed and unemployed) with severe disabilities reported that they

Figure 3.12

Percentage of persons with disabilities who worked 30 hours per week* or more, by severity, 1991

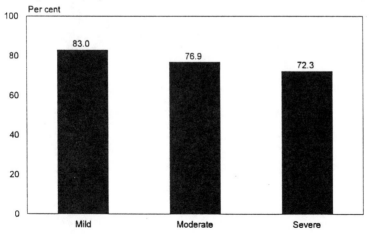

*Includes persons in the labour force who reported working at least one hour a week
See "Presentation of data" in Chapter 1 for assumptions used.

required a modified work schedule, compared to only 7 per cent of those with mild disabilities (not illustrated). Unfortunately, there is no way of knowing the extent of the modifications required; they may have been as slight as longer lunch breaks or as great as working only a few hours a week.

Slightly more information is available about those who were unemployed. About 31 per cent of unemployed persons with mild disabilities and nearly 29 per cent of unemployed persons with severe disabilities reported that they were seeking part-time work. Level of severity of the disability seemed to have almost no effect with respect to choosing to seek part-time employment.

A bigger difference lies in the percentage of persons willing to take either full-time or part-time employment. Unemployed persons with severe disabilities were more likely to accept either part-time or full-time work (27 per cent would have taken either) than persons with mild disabilities (18 per cent would have taken either). As well, more unemployed persons with mild disabilities were seeking only full-time employment (51 per cent) than was the case for unemployed persons with severe disabilities (44 per cent) (not illustrated).

The second plausible explanation for the higher rate of part-time work among persons with severe disabilities involves the hiring practices of employers. Employers may be less likely to consider persons with severe disabilities for full-time employment, although this cannot be examined with the present data.

In spite of the differences in full-time employment among employed persons with disabilities with varying levels of severity, it is important to note that even among those with severe disabilities, the majority who were working did so on a full-time basis in 1991.

Disability type and the number of hours worked per week

Given the high rate of labour force participation among persons with hearing and unknown physical disabilities, it should be no surprise that employed persons with these two types of disabilities were the most likely to be working full-time. In 1991, among those who were employed, 87.1 per cent of those with hearing disabilities and 84.1 per cent of those with unknown physical disabilities were employed 30 hours per week or more (not illustrated). Close behind were employed persons with seeing disabilities, 83.2 per cent of whom worked full-time.[10]

Besides having the highest unemployment rate, persons with mental/learning disabilities were the least likely to be employed full-time when they did find a job,[11] with 73.8 per cent working 30 hours per week or more (not illustrated).They were also among those most likely to report a requirement for modified work schedules. Nearly 12 per cent of all persons with disabilities in the labour force reported that they needed to modify their work schedule, while nearly 16 per cent of persons with mental/learning disabilities made this claim (not illustrated). However, unemployed persons with mental/learning disabilities were not obviously more likely to be seeking part-time work. Among all unemployed persons with disabilities, almost 29 per cent reported that they were looking for part-time work. About 30 per cent of those with mental/learning disabilities wanted part-time work (not illustrated).

From this information, it is difficult to know whether the greater incidence of part-time work among persons with

---

10. Persons with seeing disabilities had the lowest labour force participation rate in 1986. In 1991, they were participating slightly more in comparison with those with other types of disabilities, but they were still not among those most likely to participate. However, those who were in the labour force had a relatively low rate of unemployment (the third lowest in 1991 behind hearing and unknown physical disabilities) and a high rate of working full-time (the third highest behind hearing and unknown physical disabilities). Even persons with severe seeing disabilities had a fairly high rate of working full-time relative to others with severe disabilities.

11. This occurred within every level of severity.

mental/learning disabilities was because of choices they made or because employers were less likely to consider such individuals for full-time work.

Education and the number of hours worked per week

As already indicated, higher education typically gives an employment advantage to people with disabilities. However, while those with higher education generally had greater labour force participation and lower rates of unemployment, among those employed in 1991 there was only a slight connection between educational attainment and the likelihood of working full-time.

When students were excluded from the analysis,[12] the percentages of persons with disabilities working full-time were fairly similar, regardless of their level of education – unless they had trades certification. These percentages ranged from 82.2 per cent working full-time for those who had not finished high school to 83.9 per cent working full-time for those who had completed post-secondary school. Only those with trades certificates were noticeably more likely than the rest to be working full-time, with 88.5 per cent doing so in 1991 (not illustrated).

Reviewing the figures for men compared to women sheds more light on this. About 93 per cent of men with disabilities who had either trades certificates or post-secondary credentials worked full-time. About 91 per cent of men with disabilities whose highest level of education was high school or less worked full-time. Thus, for men with disabilities, level of educational attainment had a

---

12. A high proportion of persons aged 15 to 24 working part-time were doing so because they were still enrolled in high school or post-secondary school. With their education yet incomplete, any link between their highest level of education and their likelihood of working full-time depended on their status as a student. Removing these individuals from the analysis gives a more realistic view of the relationship between educational attainment and the likelihood of working full-time.

negligible effect on the likelihood of full-time employment (not illustrated).

Women with disabilities whose highest level of education was high school or higher also showed only a slight variation in working full-time (from 74 to 76 per cent).[13] However, women with disabilities who had not completed high school were noticeably less likely to be employed full-time. Only about 67 per cent of women with disabilities who had not completed high school worked full-time (not illustrated). Among persons with disabilities, therefore, level of education had a notable impact on full-time employment only for women without high school diplomas.

From the data available, it is difficult to determine how much of the differences in full-time employment among these groups were due to individual choice or to decisions made by employers. While more people with severe and mental/learning disabilities needed modified work schedules, unemployed members of both these groups reported wanting full-time work as much as any other group.

The distinction between part-time and full-time work is important in an economic profile. Individuals working full-time hours typically earn much more than those working part-time hours. In 1991, this was true for both persons with and without disabilities. Factors that have an impact on the likelihood of full-time work, therefore, also have an indirect impact on earnings. In the next section, earnings – one of the major indicators of economic success in the labour market – are examined.

---

13. This includes those with trades certificates. However, the vast majority of all employed persons with disabilities who had trades certificates were men. Since men were also more likely to work full-time than women, it appeared that those with trades certificates in general had higher rates of full-time employment.

Disability and the earnings gap

Earnings from employment represent the most significant source of income for adults under the age of 65 with disabilities. Whether or not an individual will have earnings is affected by a number of factors. These include the variables that influence labour force participation as well as unemployment and the amount of time a person actually spends on the job. For those people with disabilities who are able to find employment, the earnings they receive also depend upon a number of variables.

Given the labour force disadvantages already described for persons with disabilities, it is no surprise that persons with disabilities generally earned less in 1991 than those without disabilities. Nonetheless, the distribution of persons with and without disabilities throughout the different levels of earnings was more similar than might be expected.

Figure 3.13 shows that persons without disabilities were more likely than those with disabilities to be in the highest earnings bracket ($35,000 per year or more) and less likely to be in the lowest earnings bracket (less than $5,000 per year).[14] But these differences were modest. For example, 27.3 per cent of persons without disabilities earned $35,000 or more per year, compared to 23.5 per cent of persons with disabilities. Similarly, 12.8 per cent of persons without disabilities earned less than $5,000 per year, compared to 14.8 per cent of those with disabilities. Before drawing any conclusions about the differences in the earnings distributions of persons with and without disabilities, however, consider the following.

From the 1991 HALS data available for public use, there is no way to know where most individuals were located in

---

14. These are in 1991 dollars, not adjusted.

the earnings categories presented.[15] It is possible that most people with disabilities in the $25,000 to $34,999 earnings category may have actually earned just slightly more than $25,000, while most of those without disabilities may have actually earned closer to the upper limit of $34,999. In other words, there could have been significant differences between persons with and without disabilities within the same earnings category.

It might be more precise to compare *average* earnings. *A Portrait of Persons with Disabilities* provides measures of the "average employment income" for people aged 15 to 64 both with and without disabilities.[16] The average earnings of persons with disabilities was $22,055, and for those without disabilities, $25,405. This indicates that those with

Figure 3.13

Distribution of earnings* for persons with and without disabilities, 1991

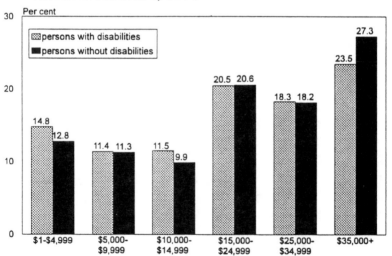

*for those who were in the labour force and had some earnings
See "Presentation of data" in Chapter 1 for assumptions used.

---

15. While more precise (continuous level) earnings data were gathered by the HALS, the data available to the public (in public-use tapes) include levels of earnings by category only, not *within* categories. The more precise data were used by Statistics Canada in *A Portrait of Persons with Disabilities* to calculate average earnings.

16. Statistics Canada, 1995, p. 65. Actual dollar values for earnings are required for the calculation of averages.

disabilities earned roughly 87 per cent of what those without disabilities earned in 1991.

It is important to note that the rate of disability increases with age. Therefore, people with disabilities tend to be older than those without disabilities. This is true of those both in and out of the labour force.[17] Also, the youngest persons (with and without disabilities) tend to have the lowest earnings. This means that the people with disabilities included a higher proportion of older persons whose earnings potential was at its peak, and that the people without disabilities included a relatively higher proportion whose earnings potential was at its lowest. If the age composition of the two groups had been more similar, the gap in earnings might have been larger.[18]

The data presented in Figure 3.13 and the average earnings figures provided by Statistics Canada include both part-time and full-time workers. As illustrated in Figure 3.14, there were large differences in the earnings of full-time and part-time workers. For example, 37.6 per cent of part-time workers earned less than $5,000, compared to only 9 per cent of those working full-time (30 hours per week or more). At the same time, 51.6 per cent of full-time workers earned $25,000 or more, compared to only 9.3 per cent of part-time workers. As noted in the previous section, persons with disabilities were somewhat more likely to work part-time than persons without disabilities. To standardize the remainder of the analysis of earnings in this section, only persons working full-time (30 hours per week or more) are

---

17. Among those working full-time (30 hours per week or more) with some earnings, the age distributions were as follows. For persons with disabilities: 15 to 24, 8.6 per cent; 25 to 44, 50.3 per cent; 45 to 64, 41.1 per cent. For persons without disabilities: 15 to 24, 13.2 per cent; 25 to 44, 60.9 per cent; 45 to 64, 25.9 per cent.

18. If persons without disabilities had an age distribution like that of persons with disabilities (that is, a higher proportion of older individuals), the overall average earnings for persons aged 15 to 64 without disabilities could be estimated at $28,045, assuming each age group maintained the average earnings cited above. This would mean that the average earnings of persons with disabilities would fall from 87 per cent to 79 per cent of that of persons without disabilities (adjusting for differences in the age composition of the two groups).

Figure 3.14

Distribution of earnings* for persons with disabilities by full-time and part-time status, 1991

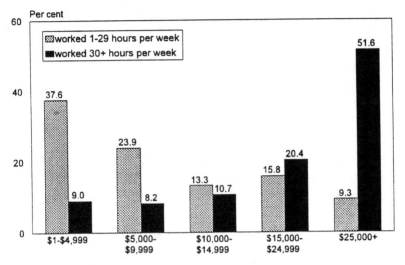

*for those who were in the labour force and had some earnings
See "Presentation of data" in Chapter 1 for assumptions used.

Figure 3.15

Distribution of earnings* for persons with and without disabilities who worked 30 hours per week or more, 1991

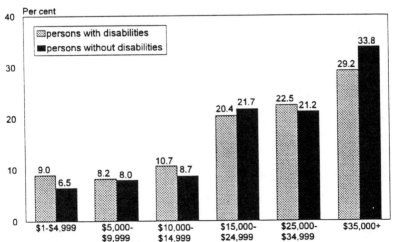

*for those who were in the labour force and had some earnings
See "Presentation of data" in Chapter 1 for assumptions used.

considered. This allows an examination of the effects of a number of variables on people's earnings without the complication of the differences in the number of hours they worked.

When only those working full-time were considered, the comparison of earnings of people with and without disabilities indicated that only small differences in the earnings distribution existed between them (Figure 3.15).

Factors affecting earnings of persons with disabilities

As noted in *An Economic Profile of Persons with Disabilities in Canada*, a multitude of factors influence the earnings of persons with disabilities and many of them are difficult to measure.[19] These include factors such as intelligence, talent, determination, personality, creativity, support from others, support from specific programs, discrimination and sheer luck. A number of variables can be measured, however, and the following sections highlight the effects of these variables on earnings.[20]

Education and earnings

Figure 3.16 illustrates the effect of one's level of education on earnings for adults with disabilities working full-time. For ease of presentation, the earnings categories have been collapsed into three groups: $1 to $24,999; $25,000 to $34,999; and $35,000 or more.

The benefits of trades certification and post-secondary credentials are obvious. Of those people with disabilities whose highest level of education was completed high school, only 22.9 per cent earned $35,000 or more, while about twice that many with post-secondary credentials (43.5 per cent) were in that earnings bracket. At the other end of the earnings spectrum, 55.5 per cent of those with

---

19. Ross and Shillington, 1990.
20. See Appendix C for additional analysis of these variables and earnings using multiple regression.

completed high school earned less than $25,000, compared to only 37.1 per cent of those with post-secondary qualifications.[21] People with trades certification earned more than those with high school or less, but not as much as those with post-secondary credentials. Figure 3.16 also indicates that there was little difference in the earnings prospects of those who completed high school and those who did not.[22]

Figure 3.16

Distribution of earnings* for persons with disabilities who worked 30 hours per week or more, by highest level of education, 1991

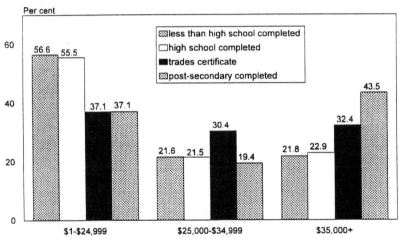

*for those who were in the labour force and had some earnings
See "Presentation of data" in Chapter 1 for assumptions used.

---

21. Among people without disabilities working full-time, 48.2 per cent of those with post-secondary qualifications earned $35,000 or more; 35.6 per cent of those with trades certification earned $35,000 or more; and 24.2 per cent and 21.5 per cent of those with completed high school and less than completed high school, respectively, were in this earnings bracket.

22. This type of analysis often fails to detect some of the nuances of the relationship between two variables. Regression analysis (see Appendix C) indicated that, when a number of other variables were controlled (such as occupation, severity, training, age, sex, etc.), people with disabilities who had obtained a high school diploma did benefit in their earnings more than those who had not. But this benefit was not as large as that enjoyed by persons who had completed either trades certification or post-secondary education.

Work-related training and earnings

The earnings advantage of work-related training for persons with disabilities is evident in Figure 3.17. Among those working full-time, 37.3 per cent of those who had work-related training earned $35,000 or more per year, compared to only 21.6 per cent of those who did not have such training. Conversely, 61 per cent of those who did not have work-related training earned less than $25,000, compared to only 34.8 per cent of those with such training.

Education and work-related training

Educational attainment is linked to work-related training. People with disabilties who attained higher levels of education also had a greater likelihood of having work-related training. Figure 3.18 shows that 63.7 per cent of persons with disabilities who had post-secondary credentials and were working full-time had work-related training. Trades certification and post-secondary credentials were almost equally likely to lead to work-related training, while only 45.5 per cent of those who had completed high school had such training. Nevertheless, a person with a high school diploma definitely had a training advantage over those who did not. Fewer than 28.1 per cent of those who had not completed high school had such training. Higher levels of education led to a greater likelihood of work-related training for people with disabilities; and, as outlined in the previous section, work-related training was associated with higher levels of earnings. Therefore, in addition to having a direct effect on earnings, education also influenced earnings through training opportunities.[23]

Occupational group and earnings

Certain occupations were more likely to provide higher levels of earnings than others. Of the six occupational categories considered here, professionals/managers had the highest earnings. Professionals and managers enjoyed a substantial earnings premium, and supervisors/forewomen

---

23. Similar conclusions can be drawn from the regression analysis summarized in Appendix C.

Figure 3.17
Distribution of earnings* for persons with disabilities who worked 30 hours per week or more, by work-related training, 1991

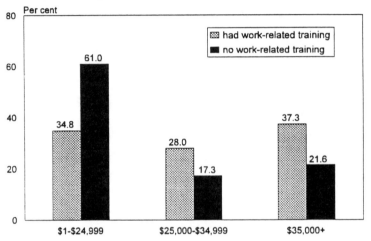

*for those who were in the labour force and had some earnings
See "Presentation of data" in Chapter 1 for assumptions used.

Figure 3.18
Percentage of persons with disabilities* working 30 hours per week or more who had work-related training, by highest level of education, 1991

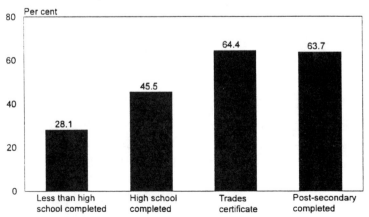

*for those who were in the labour force and had some earnings
See "Presentation of data" in Chapter 1 for assumptions used.

and foremen ranked a close second. Semi-professionals and technicians were next in terms of earning potential, followed by blue-collar workers.[24] Clerical workers and sales/service workers had the lowest earning potential of all.

Illustrating the complete range of differences in earnings among persons with disabilities in the various occupational categories is not easy. To simplify, only the percentage of persons in the highest earnings category ($35,000 or more) by each occupational grouping is presented in Figure 3.19.

This figure shows that nearly half of all full-time professionals/managers with disabilities earned $35,000 or more. Only 10.7 per cent of full-time clerical workers with disabilities were in this earnings bracket. While it might seem from Figure 3.19 that clerical workers were somewhat worse off than sales/service workers, it is important to know that at the other end of the earnings spectrum (those

Figure 3.19

Percentage of persons with disabilities* working 30 hours per week or more who earned $35,000 per year or more, by occupational group, 1991

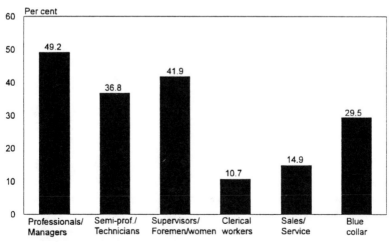

*for those were in the labour force and had some earnings
See "Presentation of data" in Chapter 1 for assumptions used.

24. In Appendix C, however, it is evident that male blue-collar workers had much higher earnings than their female counterparts.

earning under $25,000), sales/service workers were actually more highly represented. In other words, a higher percentage of sales/service workers than clerical workers earned $35,000 or more. However, a higher percentage of sales/service workers than clerical workers also earned less than $25,000. The other end of the earnings spectrum is summarized in Figure 3.20.[25]

Figure 3.20

Percentage of persons with disabilities* working 30 hours per week or more who earned less than $25,000 per year, by occupational group, 1991

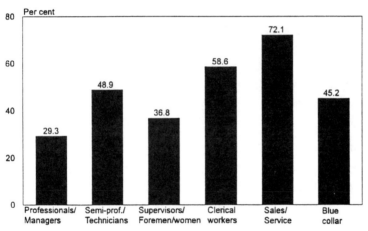

*for those who were in the labour force and had some earnings
See "Presentation of data" in Chapter 1 for assumptions used.

Sex and earnings

The earnings disadvantage experienced by women with disabilities working full-time is abundantly evident in Figure 3.21. Only 14.3 per cent of these women earned $35,000 or more. More than twice that percentage (37.9 per cent) of their male counterparts earned $35,000 or more. At the other end of the spectrum, 65.6 per cent of these women earned under $25,000, compared to only 38.4 per cent of their male counterparts.

---

25.   Although not shown here, higher levels of education were found to be associated with the more lucrative occupational categories. Education, therefore, also has an indirect effect on earnings through occupation. This finding is reflected in the regression analysis summarized in Appendix C.

Not only were women with disabilities less likely than men with disabilities to be in the labour force, more likely to be unemployed and less likely to work full-time hours when employed, they also had lower earnings when they worked full-time.[26]

Figure 3.21

Distribution of earnings* for persons with disabilities working 30 hours per week or more, by sex, 1991

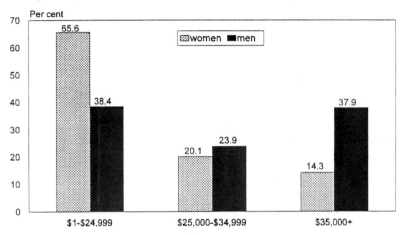

*for those who were in the labour force and had some earnings
See "Presentation of data" in Chapter 1 for assumptions used.

Age and earnings

The much lower levels of earnings associated with young people (aged 15 to 24) with disabilities working full-time is captured in Figure 3.22. An overwhelming majority of them (90.5 per cent) earned less than $25,000. About half that percentage of the two older age groups were in this earnings bracket. Since these figures include only those working full-time, the greater tendency of young people to work part-time (often while going to school) was not a factor in these findings. However, the results are not very different from those for persons without disabilities. Among those

---

26. See the results of regression analysis in Appendix C for an estimate of the "earnings penalty" experienced by women with disabilities net of the effect of the other variables.

aged 15 to 24 without disabilities working full-time, 87.2 per cent earned less than $25,000 (not illustrated). These findings suggest a phenomenon common to all young people, regardless of disability status.

Earnings potential seems to improve with age. Among people aged 45 to 64 with disabilities, 34.5 per cent earned $35,000 or more. Somewhat fewer, 29.6 per cent, of those aged 25 to 44 were in this highest earnings bracket. As noted in Chapter 2, people with disabilities in the oldest age group (45 to 64) were less likely to participate in the labour force. However, for those who did and had full-time employment, the potential for higher earnings was greater than at any other age.

Figure 3.22

Distribution of earnings* for persons with disabilities working 30 hours per week or more, by age group, 1991

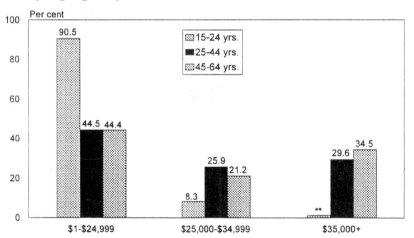

* for those who were in the labour force and had some earnings
** sample size too small to release percentage
See "Presentation of data" in Chapter 1 for assumptions used.

Severity of the disability and earnings

People with mild disabilities were more likely to participate in the labour force, more likely to be employed once they were in the labour force, and more likely to work full-time than those with moderate or severe disabilities. It is no surprise, then, that persons with mild disabilities also tended to earn more than those with more severe disabilities. Among persons with mild disabilities working full-time, 30.7 per cent earned $35,000 or more. About a quarter of all persons with moderate disabilities earned that much, and only slightly more than a fifth of those with severe disabilities did[27] (Figure 3.23).

Figure 3.23

Distribution of earnings* for persons with disabilities working 30 hours per week or more, by severity of disability, 1991

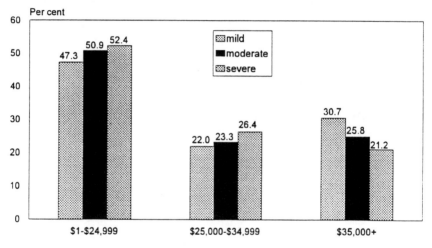

*for those who were in the labour force and had some earnings
See "Presentation of data" in Chapter 1 for assumptions used.

---

27. The regression analysis summarized in Appendix C revealed that when all other variables were considered, severity did not have as great an effect on earnings as one might expect. This is probably because severity also affected some of the other variables critical to earnings, such as education, occupation and training. The relationship between severity and earnings depicted in Figure 3.23 does not take into account the role of any other variables.

Disability type and earnings

People with unknown physical disabilities and hearing disabilities were more likely to participate in the labour force, less likely to be unemployed and more likely to work full-time. Their labour force advantage over those with other disability types also extended to earnings potential.

As with the relationship between occupation and earnings, the relationship between a person's disability type and their earnings is difficult to show graphically in a single figure. Thus, this relationship is summarized in two separate graphs: one showing the percentage of persons with each disability type who earned $35,000 or more (33.5 per cent), and another showing the percentage of persons with each disability type who earned less than $25,000.

Persons with unknown physical disabilities had the highest percentage earning $35,000 or more (38.9 per cent); those with hearing disabilities had the second highest percentage earning $35,000 or more (33.5 per cent); and

Figure 3.24

Percentage of persons with disabilities* working 30 hours per week or more who earned $35,000 per year or more, by disability type, 1991

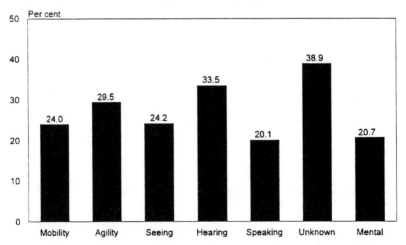

*for those who were in the labour force and had some earnings
See "Presentation of data" in Chapter 1 for assumptions used.

those with agility disabilities ranked third (29.5 per cent). Persons with either mental/learning or speaking disabilities had the lowest percentage in this highest earnings bracket (20.7 per cent and 20.1 per cent respectively) (Figure 3.24).

At the other end of the earnings spectrum, people with unknown physical disabilities and hearing disabilities had the lowest percentage of those who earned less than $25,000, at 39.4 per cent and 41.4 per cent respectively. Those with speaking disabilities, at 66.1 per cent, were the most likely to have had earnings under $25,000 (Figure 3.25).

With the highest unemployment rate, the highest rate of part-time work and the lowest earnings potential, persons with mental/learning disabilities seemed to face the greatest disadvantage of all others with disabilities – in spite of having a relatively high rate of labour force participation.

Figure 3.25

Percentage of persons with disabilities* working 30 hours per week or more who earned less than $25,000 per year, by disability type, 1991

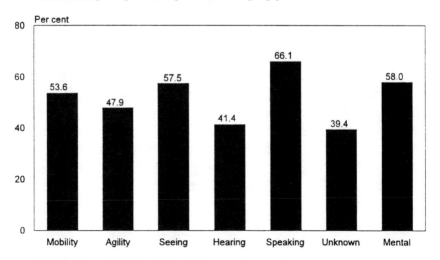

*for those who were in the labour force and had some earnings
See "Presentation of data" in Chapter 1 for assumptions used.

Discussion

One of the greatest challenges facing persons with disabilities who were in the labour force was finding employment. In 1991 in Canada, the unemployment rate of persons without disabilities was 9.8 per cent. The unemployment rate for persons with disabilities was almost one and a half times as much, at 14.4 per cent.

The initial hurdle of finding a job was a greater challenge for some groups with disabilities than others. Women, young people, those with more severe disabilities, those with mental/learning disabilities, and those with special requirements, such as accessible transportation, modified work schedules or a redesign of their job, seemed to have greater difficulty finding employment. Among some of these more disadvantaged groups, more than a quarter of those in the labour force were out of work. For example, between 27 and 29 per cent of those with either severe disabilities or special requirements were unemployed in 1991. It is not difficult to imagine that many individuals facing continual unemployment become so discouraged that they leave the labour force altogether. The low rates of labour force participation of many of these people may be inextricably linked to such discouraging employment prospects.

People who are disadvantaged in terms of finding employment can be grouped according to characteristics such as their age and sex, as well as various aspects of their disabilty, such as its severity, its type and the special requirements it demands. Besides the disadvantages that often flow from these characteristics, a number of other factors affected success in finding employment. The most significant of these was level of education.

In Chapter 2, education was found to be one of the best mechanisms available to persons with disabilities for increasing their labour force participation. The findings in this chapter indicate that the beneficial effects of education carry over into the labour force by improving one's chances of actually finding employment. For example, 10 per cent of persons with disabilities who had post-secondary credentials were unemployed, compared to nearly twice that percentage (18.5 per cent) who had not completed high school. As well, higher levels of education led to different occupational categories. For example, post-secondary credentials were much more likely than any other level of education to lead to professional and managerial occupations, which also happened to have the lowest rate of unemployment (only 6.8 per cent in 1991).

Despite what some might think, the vast majority of persons with disabilities in the labour force either had or wanted full-time work. While persons with disabilities were less likely than persons without disabilities to work full-time, the difference was actually very slight; 82.9 per cent of persons without disabilities worked full-time (30 hours per week or more), compared to 80.9 per cent of persons with disabilities. Certainly, working full-time is more financially lucrative; more than half of all persons with disabilities employed full-time earned $25,000 or more, while fewer than 10 per cent of those working part-time did. Thus, factors that contributed to the likelihood of being employed full-time also contributed to economic security.

Part-time employment was more prevalent among persons requiring special accommodations, those with severe disabilities and those with mental/learning disabilities. However, it is not clear whether this higher rate of part-time employment was voluntary or involuntary. Were persons in these groups more likely to choose part-time employment because of certain aspects of their disability or family responsibilities, or were they more likely to face fewer opportunities for full-time employment because of barriers in the workplace or the attitudes of employers?

Among persons with severe disabilities (who had one of the highest rates of part-time employment) a higher than average proportion also reported that they had to have a modified work schedule. There is no way of knowing from the available data just how great these schedule modifications might have been. Some could have been as slight as requiring an extra few minutes for lunch, more frequent breaks, starting and finishing at a different time than others in the workplace (possibly to accommodate special transit schedules) or slightly shorter work days. It is possible for a full-time work schedule to easily accommodate such requirements. On the other hand, some schedule modifications could have been as extreme as being able to work only a few hours a week.

From the information available for those who were unemployed, it is clear that persons with severe disabilities who were out of work reported wanting full-time work as much as anyone else. Nevertheless, they may have been more willing than unemployed persons with milder disabilities to take part-time work, if nothing else was available.

Earnings represented the most significant source of income for adults under 65 with disabilities. Yet, to obtain earnings, they had to first face two challenges: entering the labour force and finding employment. In Chapter 2 and in the first sections of this chapter, a number of factors were examined which had an impact on the likelihood of success in meeting these two challenges.

For those who did enter the labour force and found employment, a number of factors influenced the level of earnings attainable. While adults with disabilities had lower levels of earnings than those without disabilities, the gap among those working full-time was not as great as one might expect, given the size of the participation and unemployment gaps. However, the gap definitely existed. Persons with disabilities consistently earned less than those without disabilities, even when they had similar levels of education or were employed in similar occupations.

Education was an extremely important factor affecting earnings for persons with disabilities. Besides being one of the best ways for persons with disabilities to enhance their labour force participation, education was found to be extremely important for success in getting a job, once a person was in the labour force. Persons with disabilities who had higher levels of education were also much more likely to have had work-related training, and those with work-related training had higher levels of earnings. Similarly, higher levels of education were much more likely to lead to employment in occupational groups like professionals and managers or supervisors, forewomen and foremen, all of which produced higher levels of earnings.

While the overall educational attainment of working-age persons with disabilities increased between 1986 and 1991, this population still had lower levels of education than their counterparts without disabilities. For example, among persons working full-time with some earnings, 32.7 per cent of those with disabilities and 22.7 per cent of those without disabilities had not completed high school. Similarly, a higher proportion of persons without disabilities had completed post-secondary credentials (36.6 per cent) than those with disabilities (24.6 per cent)(not illustrated). While a continued increase in the level of education among persons with disabilities would likely lead to higher levels of earnings – not to mention greater labour force participation and lower unemployment – persons with disabilities tended to earn less than those without disabilities, even when both had the same education.

Increasing levels of education, work-related training and employment in certain occupations can all be thought of as mechanisms for improving the earnings potential of persons with disabilities. However, some characteristics of individuals themselves, such as sex and age, had a noticeable effect on earnings. Being a woman with a disability had a negative impact on earnings that cannot be explained by differences in

education, training or occupational group.[28] (Of course,
women in the general population also faced lower
earning prospects). As well, as in the general population,
young people with disabilities had much lower levels of
earnings, even when employed full-time.

It is evident in this chapter and in the previous one that
education provides a number of labour force advantages for
persons with disabilities. As discussed in the next chapter,
this population has great labour force potential – investment
in that potential through education and training can make a
difference. However, increasing the education and training
of persons with disabilities is only part of the equation.
Persons with disabilities need jobs which make use of their
education and training. Yet they often face barriers when
trying to obtain such jobs.

About a third of those persons with disabilities who were
employed by other people felt that their jobs did not make
use of their skills and education (not illustrated). Some
groups were more likely than others to feel underutilized,
and these tended to be the same as those who faced the
greatest challenges in the labour force in general. For
example, persons with severe rather than mild disabilities
were more likely to feel that their skills and education were
being wasted. Women with disabilities were slightly more
likely than men to make this claim. Young people with
disabilities, in particular, felt they were unable to make full
use of their skills and education; in fact, nearly half of those
aged 15 to 24 who were working for others felt this way.
While this situation improved with age, a quarter of those
aged 45 to 64 also felt underutilized on the job.[29]

---

28. This is most clearly illustrated in the regression analysis
    summarized in Appendix C where the effect of being a woman on
    earnings is measured net of an assortment of other variables (such
    as education, training, occupational category).

29. Employment in professional/managerial occupations seemed to
    reduce this feeling of underutilization; 17 per cent of persons with
    disabilities in those occupations reported such a feeling. The
    situation was less enviable for those in some other occupations,
    such as sales and service jobs, where feelings of being
    underutilized were reported by 44 per cent.

This information suggests there is a great deal of untapped potential among persons with disabilities presently in the labour force. The following chapter focusses on working-age persons with disabilities who were not in the labour force. There is also evidence of untapped potential among this group, and this evidence will be examined in the next chapter.

Chapter 4

Out of the labour force:
Untapped potential

In this chapter, persons with disabilities who were of working age but were not in the labour force are examined. There is a common misconception that persons with disabilities who are not in the labour force are either unable or unwilling to work. There is ample evidence to suggest, however, that neither perception accurately characterizes this population.

According to the 1991 HALS, there appears to have been great potential and willingness for employment among persons with disabilities who were not in the labour force. A substantial number of these persons were likely to have been part of the "hidden unemployed"[1] or persons temporarily out of the labour market. Evidence suggests that it would be unwise to write off this population as "unemployable." Many persons with disabilities were outside

---

1. These are persons who would like to have a job, but are so discouraged by dismal prospects that they have given up trying to find employment.

the labour force, not because their disability prevented them from working, but because the labour market environment produced handicap situations.

In the first section of this chapter, a number of indicators of willingness and ability to work among persons with disabilities who were out of the labour force are examined. In the second, indicators of environmental barriers are presented and added to the work potential indicators. In the third section, the meaning of an individual's self-assessed "ability to work" is examined in light of the findings of the first two sections. Finally, changes in disability status and work limitations over time are discussed.

Willingness and ability to work

From the available data, it is not possible to accurately determine the full labour market potential of those persons with disabilities who were not participating in the labour force at the time of the survey. However, the HALS included a number of questions that can be used as indicators of an individual's willingness or ability to work. Although these indicators are not exhaustive, they do provide some idea of the minimum potential for future labour force participation among this population. In this section, the indicators will be discussed individually, then a composite measure of all indicators will be examined.

Volunteer work: the unpaid labour force

One indicator of an individual's willingness and ability to work in the paid labour force is their work performance in the unpaid labour force. While individuals volunteer for a variety of reasons, many acquire useful job skills and experience that can enhance their prospects for participating in the paid labour force.[2] About 20 per cent of persons with disabilities

---

2.   Ross and Shillington, 1989.

who were out of the labour force in 1991 were active in the unpaid labour force of volunteer workers.[3]

And while some forms of volunteer work might not require skills that are transferable to the paid labour force, nearly 57 per cent of volunteers with disabilities who were out of the labour force reported that the skills they used in their volunteer work would be useful in finding future paid employment. This means that about 11 per cent[4] of persons with disabilities who were out of the labour force had skills honed through volunteer work that were directly transferable to the paid labour market (Figure 4.1). It can be argued that through their volunteer work, this 11 per cent demonstrated both a willingness and an ability to work in the paid labour force.

Figure 4.1

Volunteer experience and aquisition of job skills among persons with disabilities not in the labour force, 1991

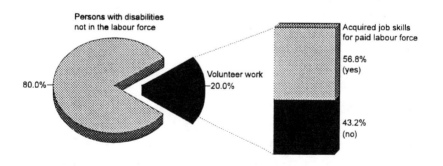

See "Presentation of data" in Chapter 1 for assumptions used.

---

3.   Findings from the 1987 Survey of Volunteer Activity in Canada revealed that one-quarter of all Canadians aged 15 and over who were not in the paid labour force reported volunteer activities (Ross and Shillington, 1989).

4.   Fifty-seven per cent of 20 per cent is 11 per cent (.57 x .2 = .11).

Students

A number of persons with disabilities were not in the labour force because they were still pursuing their education. Their status of "not in the labour force" does not indicate either an inability or an unwillingness to work for pay; rather, it indicates that they were still in a preparatory stage before entering the labour force. Nearly 10 per cent of persons with disabilities who were not in the paid labour force in 1991 were students, and the vast majority of these were under 25 years of age.[5]

Intent to look for work

One of the strongest indicators of work potential is a person's expressed intention to look for work in the future. About 17 per cent of persons with disabilities who were not in the paid labour force in 1991 reported that they intended to look for a job within the next six months. These individuals may have been waiting for their personal circumstances to change – for example, an improvement in a medical condition, graduation from school, or being relieved of a family responsibility, such as the care of young children about to start school – or, they may simply have been willing to again try their luck at finding a job.

Other indicators of the "hidden unemployed"

As mentioned, some individuals are out of the paid labour force simply because they have given up trying to find employment. These are people who want to work for pay, but they have become so discouraged about not finding a job that instead of remaining unemployed over a long

---

5.   A small proportion of students were enrolled in special schools which may have focussed on basic life skills rather than on helping students prepare to enter the labour force. However, about 90 per cent of all students indicated that they were enrolled in regular schools, colleges and universities; 80 per cent of those in regular schools (below post-secondary level) took only regular classes and another 13 per cent took a combination of regular, remedial and special classes. Even among those who attended remedial and special classes, 80 per cent took academic subjects and 37 per cent took trades or vocational training.

period, they drop out of the labour force altogether. The most obvious sign of this hidden unemployment is evidence of unsuccessful attempts to gain employment, followed by withdrawal from the labour force altogether. According to the HALS, 3.8 per cent of persons with disabilities who were out of the labour force in 1991 had looked for work over the previous two years, despite the fact that they had not been employed in the paid labour force for at least the last five years. As well, 3.4 per cent of persons with disabilities who were out of the labour force reported that they had looked for work during the previous five years, but had been turned down because of their disability.[6] It can be argued that these individuals wanted to be in the labour force, but they had become discouraged by their lack of success in finding paid work.

A composite measure of work potential

Each of the preceding characteristics can be considered as an indicator of future work potential. To get some idea of the overall potential for persons with disabilities to enter the paid labour market in the future, these indicators were combined. (There is a certain amount of overlap among the indicators, however, such as persons working as volunteers who said that they would also be looking for paid work in the next six months.) A composite measure was developed by determining whether or not an individual had a positive response to at least one of the indicators. After doing so, it appears that 30.8 per cent of persons with disabilities who were out of the paid labour force had a positive response to at least one of the five indicators of future work potential.[7] This does not mean that the remainder had no work

---

6. It was the reported belief of these individuals that they were denied employment because of their disability.

7. These individuals were: (1) doing volunteer work requiring skills useful in the paid labour market; (2) students; (3) intending to look for work in the next six months; (4) had not worked for pay in at least five years, but had looked for work without success during the last two years; or (5) had not worked for pay in at least five years, but had looked within the last five years but been turned down because of their disability.

potential, simply that there were obvious indicators available for only about 31 per cent.[8]

Persons with disabilities who were out of the paid labour force but gave some indication of work potential were more likely to be women than men (33 per cent of the women had at least one of the indicators mentioned, compared to 28 per cent of the men). As well, persons with mild disabilities were more likely to have some sign of work potential (39.5 per cent) than those with either moderate (28.7 per cent) or severe (21.1 per cent) disabilities.

Environmental barriers

In addition to the indicators of future work potential examined in the previous section, some individuals reported in the HALS that they were prevented from looking for work by circumstances other than the disability itself or by environmental factors which acted as barriers. Presumably in these cases, a change of circumstance or environment could have allowed the individual to look for work in the paid labour force. Reporting such barriers as reasons for not looking for work might be considered as additional indicators of work potential. The following provides a summary of these barriers.

Disability income and support programs

Some persons with disabilities who were out of the labour force reported that they were not looking for work for

---

8. Persons with disabilities who were out of the labour force were asked if they had ever received, or wanted to receive, work-related training. Unfortunately, it is not possible from the data to establish the temporal sequence between the onset of an individual's disability and their desire for or participation in training, in order to use this information as an indicator of work potential. If we knew, for example, that an individual had either wanted or received work-related training after their disability became apparent, this could be considered as an indicator of work potential. Regardless of the temporal sequence, however, it is interesting to note that just over one-quarter of persons with disabilities who were not in the labour force had some form of work-related training and a further 15 per cent wanted such training.

reasons that involved the disability income and support programs available at that time. For example, 21.4 per cent reported that they were afraid of losing their income support and 13 per cent said they were afraid of losing their disability supports and services such as subsidized medication, special transportation, assistive devices, medical services not covered by basic provincial health care plans, and so on, as well as other disability-related services.

In the absence of labour force earnings, many of these individuals relied on social assistance, CPP/QPP disability benefits, Workers' Compensation or private disability insurance plans for their income. These alternative sources of income will be discussed in greater detail in the next chapter; however, it is important to note here that many individuals who relied on these income sources would have had difficulty re-establishing these benefits if they had found work in the paid labour force, but then lost their job. Others realized that they would have been unable to earn enough from the labour market to both pay for the disability-related supports and services they needed and provide for their living expenses. There may be an earnings threshold for persons with disabilities – an amount of earnings below which it is impossible to provide for both basic living expenses and the extra costs of having a disability. Individuals may make a rational decision not to enter the labour force unless they can attain a certain minimum amount of earnings.

Personal situations

Other individuals reported situations in their personal lives that prevented them from looking for work. For example, 5.7 per cent had been discouraged by family or friends from seeking paid work and 10.1 per cent had family responsibilities that prevented them from seeking work in the paid labour force. (This latter group were primarily women with children under six years of age.)

The labour market

Other individuals had concerns about the environment in the labour market itself. For example, 5.8 per cent reported that they had no access to job information, 4.8 per cent worried about being isolated on the job because of their disability, 7.4 per cent had experienced past discrimination in the labour force, 7.3 per cent reported a lack of accessible transportation to get to and from work, 15.1 per cent felt there were no jobs available for them, and 16.5 per cent felt that their training was inadequate to find employment.

Environmental barriers combined

In total, 43.8 per cent of all persons with disabilities who were not in the labour force in 1991 reported that at least one environmental barrier prevented them from looking for work. The interaction of these barriers with the disability itself had created a labour force handicap for these individuals.

Environmental barriers and work potential indicators combined

The composite measure of work potential developed in the first section provides a conservative estimate of the number of individuals who showed some potential for entering the paid labour market. The composite measure of environmental barriers just cited gives another estimate of the number of individuals who might show potential for entering the paid labour force if the environmental barriers could be removed or the individual's personal circumstances (beyond the disability) were to change. Many individuals who showed future work potential according to the first set of indicators also cited at least one environmental barrier to paid employment.

These two measures − work potential and environmental barriers − can be combined to provide yet another estimate of the potential for labour force participation among this population. About 56 per cent of persons with disabilities not in the labour force either showed some sign of work potential or cited an environmental or personal barrier as the reason they were out of the labour force. This means that if circumstances (other than the disability itself) had changed, more than half of the persons with disabilities who were out of the labour force would have been likely candidates for paid employment.[9]

Self-assessed ability to work

In the 1991 HALS, persons with disabilities who were out of the paid labour force were asked whether their "condition or health problem completely prevented them from working at a job or business," or "limited the kind or amount of work they could do at a job or business."[10] There were some curious findings. For example, 52.5 per cent of those who reported that they were prevented from working also showed some sign of future work potential, or they cited an environmental barrier as the reason they were out of the labour force. An individual's self-assessed ability – or inability – to work, therefore, seems to depend on the nature of the disability, as well as environmental factors and life circumstances. Thus, a change in the disability or a change in an individual's environment or life circumstances could allow them to enter the paid labour force. This could account for the fact that 11 per cent of those who reported that they were completely prevented from working also reported that they intended to look for work within the following six months. While this may seem like a contradiction, it merely captures those who expected a change in either their condition or their environment in the near future.

---

9. Fewer than five per cent of persons with disabilities who were out of the paid labour force showed absolutely no sign of potential involvement (past, present or future). These individuals had never worked, did not indicate having ever looked for work, were not students, did not report doing volunteer work in the past year, did not intend to look for work in the next six months, and reported that they were completely prevented from working.

10. Excerpted from the HALS questionnaire.

Disability is not a static state

As already outlined, a change in the nature or severity of an individual's disability or a change in their environment can increase their potential for labour force participation.[11] Environments and life circumstances change: students graduate, family responsibilities lighten (young children start school), education and training enhance skills which can improve employment prospects, volunteers hone their skills and make contacts that can help facilitate the move to paid employment, employers' attitudes can improve, accessibility can be enhanced, and special programs can help match an individual with a job. All these environmental changes can lead to greater labour force involvement. In addition, the disability itself can change, thus allowing greater labour force involvement. This section examines the potential for changes in disability status.

Despite the common perception that disability is primarily a static state, evidence suggests that a surprising number of persons with disabilities may, in fact, experience significant changes in their disability status from one year to the next. Because such changes can only be identified through longitudinal surveys in which the same individuals are questioned at different points in time, this section relies on data from the longitudinal Labour Market Activity Survey (LMAS) for 1989-1990.

The "disability turnover" phenomenon

Results from the LMAS indicate that only about 36 per cent of persons identified as having a disability in 1989 reported having a disability of the same severity level in 1990.[12] The remaining 64 per cent either changed severity levels – 10 per cent became more severe and 10 per cent

---

11. It can also result in a decreased potential for future labour force participation, depending on the nature of the change.

12. Differences between the LMAS and the HALS were discussed in Chapter 1. While the LMAS uses only a sub-set of HALS screening questions, it identifies the same population of persons with disabilities, and the conceptualization of severity levels is comparable in the two surveys.

became less severe – or they appeared to have a complete reversal of their disability status (44 per cent). Most surprising, of course, is the finding that 44 per cent of working-age persons who had a disability in 1989 no longer had one in 1990 (referred to as the "exiting turnover," see Figure 4.2). A similar proportion of persons who had a disability in 1990 did not have one the previous year (referred to as the "entry turnover," not illustrated), thus maintaining a fairly constant overall rate of disability from year to year in the total population.

Mild disabilities: the greatest rate of turnover

The majority of persons experiencing an exiting turnover had a mild disability in 1989 (76 per cent); 20 per cent had a moderate disability and 4 per cent had a severe disability. This is not simply because there were more people with mild disabilities than there were persons with moderate or severe disabilities. When examining only those with a mild disability in 1989, the exiting turnover rate was highest at 58 per cent. For those with moderate disabilities in 1989, 29 per cent experienced an exiting turnover, and for those with severe

Figure 4.2

Change in disability status from 1989 to 1990 for persons reporting a disability in 1989

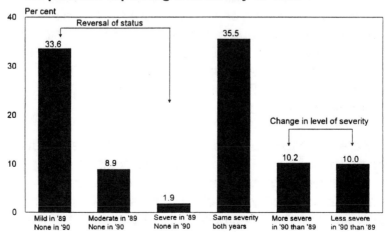

Source: Calculations by the author based on Statistics Canada's Longitudinal Person Master File from Labour Market Activity Survey (LMAS), 1989-90.

disabilities, the turnover rate was lowest at 16 per cent (not illustrated). While the turnover phenomenon is certainly more likely to affect those with mild disabilities, a reversal of disability status occurred even among those with severe disabilities.

What does this turnover phenomenon mean?

The turnover phenomenon does not necessarily mean that 44 per cent of persons with disabilities suddenly recover from their underlying condition and no longer have a disability. It merely means that the functional limitations experienced (or the perception of them) may vary from year to year.

Evidence in the LMAS indicates that those experiencing a turnover tended to have a history of disability or some underlying health problem that predated 1989. For example, among those experiencing an entry turnover (no disability in 1989, disability in 1990), 39 per cent reported noticing that their condition began to limit them at work in 1988 or earlier.

This means that about two of every five people who experienced an entry turnover in disability status reported evidence of a disability prior to 1989. They reported signs of work limitations due to a disability in 1988 or earlier, then reported no disability at all in 1989, and subsequently reported a work-limiting or work-preventing disability in 1990. For these individuals, the underlying condition may not have disappeared in 1989, but there may have been a variation in the degree to which it caused a functional limitation (disability). This evidence suggests that some disabilities may be cyclical.

There are other possible explanations for this turnover phenomenon. For example, some individuals may recover from the underlying condition or injury and no longer experience a disability. For others, the acceptance of an activity limitation may lag behind the actual onset of the limitation. Some people may have a disability for years, but only recognize their functional limitations as a result of repeated negative experiences. At that point, they may reflect on the past and remember earlier incidents that involved their limitation. As a result, an individual's memory of when a limitation began can vary over time. This may be more likely to happen when the disability in question is mild.

It may also be that some individuals had a health problem that they expected to be short-term when they answered the questionnaire in 1989. When they were resurveyed in 1990, they realized that the problem had persisted or would last longer than the six months outlined in the survey definition.[13]

Changes in disability status and the perception of work limitations

Regardless of whether we are witnessing cyclical disabilities, a true reversal in disability status, or uncertainty about the existence of a functional limitation, the turnover phenomenon provides evidence that there is at least some variation in one's perception of disability over time for a substantial number of persons with disabilities. This can be demonstrated using the LMAS by focussing on persons who reported having a disability in 1989 that either prevented them from working or limited them at work. One year later, about 10 per cent of these individuals reported that, although they still had the disability, it was not work-limiting. An additional 30 per cent reported no disability at all.[14]

Changes in the reporting of one's disability status and its impact on work involve more than just a person's perception – they are backed by changes in labour force status as well. For example, of those persons who reported having a

---

13. In both the HALS and the LMAS, an individual is not considered to have a disability if a seeing limitation can be corrected by eyeglasses or contact lenses, or if a hearing limitation can be corrected by a hearing device. Hearing disabilities had the highest rate of turnover of any disability type, and it may be that some of this turnover was due to the acquisition of some sort of hearing device.

14. Some disabilities can become work-limiting over time. Of those who reported a non-work-limiting disability in 1989, 12 per cent reported being limited by the disability the next year, 24 per cent reported the same status, and 63 per cent reported no disability at all.

work-limiting or work-preventing disability in 1989, nearly 30 per cent then worked a full year (52 weeks) in 1990. Such examples remind us that there is substantial potential for future participation in the labour force, even among those who report that their disability limits them at work or prevents them from working.

Discussion

Nearly 44 per cent of persons with disabilities were out of the paid labour force in 1991. The common perception that most of these individuals were either unable or unwilling to work is contradicted by the evidence presented in this chapter. In the HALS, about 31 per cent of persons with disabilities who were out of the paid labour force showed obvious signs of future work potential. Some worked in the unpaid labour force as volunteers, utilizing skills which could be transferred to the paid labour force. Others were students still pursuing their education, some individuals reported that they intended to look for work within six months, and some had simply given up trying to find a job in a labour market with already high rates of unemployment for persons with disabilities.

As well, nearly 44 per cent of persons with disabilities who were not in the paid labour force reported that they were prevented from looking for paid work by at least one environmental barrier or personal circumstance. Among these barriers were a lack of accessible transportation to and from work, a fear of isolation in the workplace due to the disability, lack of information about available jobs and insufficient training for them, past experiences with discrimination in the labour market due to the disability, a fear of losing disability income and supports from non-market sources, restrictive family responsibilities, and discouragement from family or friends.

The interaction between these environmental barriers and the disability itself produced work handicaps for these individuals. Lifting these barriers could easily diminish these handicapping situations and facilitate entry into the paid labour market. Overall, 56 per cent of persons with disabilities who were out of the paid labour force showed signs of future work potential or indicated that at least one environmental barrier kept them from looking for work.

In many cases, it is not the disability alone that prevents an individual from entering the labour force, it is the interaction between the disability and environmental factors. This interaction is dynamic, changing over time as both the environment and the disability change. Contrary to popular belief, a substantial amount of change in disability status may occur from one year to the next. Data from the 1989-90 LMAS indicates that close to 44 per cent of persons with disabilities in 1989 had a reversal of their disability status the following year and for 20 per cent, the severity of the disability changed. There is also evidence that many disabilities may be cyclical in nature. This means that some persons with disabilities may require temporary periods of time out of the labour force during particular stages of the cycle.

Persons with disabilities who are out of the labour force demonstrate both an ability and a willingness to work in the paid labour force. They do so through their activities while they are out of the labour force, by their past history in the labour force, and by their attempts to get back into it. Some individuals need physical accommodations to enter the labour force. Some may require disability-related supports and services, and others may require temporary absences to accommodate cyclical disabilities. Some may require extra training. All require an employer with an open mind. For persons with disabilities, finding a job may be more challenging than simply finding a match between abilities, interests, geographic location and job requirements. For some, it also means finding an accessible workplace, accessible transportation to and from work, and an employer willing to look beyond the disability.

As in the general population, a number of persons with disabilities are not in the paid labour force because they are involved in other activities. They may be students, unpaid caregivers for small children and other family members, or early retirees. And some individuals, in both the general population and among persons with disabilities, are not in the paid labour force because they lack sufficient education, training or skills to obtain paid employment. For persons with disabilities, such deficiencies are likely to have an even more dramatic and negative effect on their labour force prospects.

There is likely a relatively stable population of individuals with disabilities who have no attachment to the paid labour force. For them, the disability may be of such a nature that no existing workplace accommodations could facilitate paid work. It is impossible to determine the size of this core of individuals. Nevertheless, evidence suggests that the majority of persons with disabilities who are not in the labour force have the potential for future labour force involvement.

Chapter 5

Income sources & low income
among persons with disabilities

The previous chapters have focussed on the working-age population and labour force issues. This chapter looks at the broader economic picture by examining poverty among adults with disabilities and income sources other than earnings. A number of methods are available to define poverty.[1] The method used here relies on Statistics Canada's Low Income Cut-offs (LICOs), which are one of the most widely used and accepted measures of poverty in the area of social policy research. Persons with family incomes below the low income cut-offs are defined by Statistics Canada as living in "straitened circumstances" and in this book, are defined as "poor."[2] The low income cut-offs are based on family income and are adjusted for the size of the family and the size of the community in which they live.

---

1. For a discussion of various definitions of poverty, see Chapter 2 of Ross, Shillington and Lochhead, *The Canadian Fact Book on Poverty – 1994.*

2. Although this measure is widely used as an indicator of poverty, it is not defined as such by Statistics Canada.

Adults with disabilities are much more likely to be poor than those without disabilities. In 1991, 21.9 per cent of adults (aged 15 years and older) with disabilities were living in poverty, compared to 12.6 per cent of adults without disabilities. In the first section of this chapter, poverty rates among persons with disabilities are investigated by examining such factors as sex, age, severity, type and cause of disability, living arrangements, urban or rural residence, educational attainment, and labour force status.

It is evident that full-time employment in the paid labour market greatly decreases the chances of living in poverty for persons with disabilities. But what about the impact of other sources of income? The second section describes the disability income support system in Canada today, then examines non-market sources of income and their effect on poverty rates. In particular, the association between poverty and three specific programs is examined: social assistance, CPP/QPP disability benefits and Workers' Compensation.[3]

Poverty rates

Persons with disabilities are more likely to be poor than those without disabilities, and there are a number of factors which affect the poverty rates of persons with disabilities. Not surprisingly, most of the factors that reduce the likelihood of persons with disabilities participating in the labour force also increase the likelihood of them living in poverty. This section provides a descriptive overview of nine factors which had an impact on the poverty rates for persons with disabilities in 1991.[4]

---

3.   The number of individuals included in the HALS who received income from other non-market sources (such as private insurance, employer insurance or unemployment sickness benefits) was so low that the population estimates were unstable and could not be released.

4.   Note that the low income cut-off variable available in the HALS excluded persons living in the Northwest Territories and Yukon. For this reason, all poverty rate statistics provided in this book also exclude this population.

Sex

Women are more likely to live in poverty than men. This is true for persons with and without disabilities (Figure 5.1). However, women with disabilities are especially disadvantaged when it comes to the economic resources available to them. One-quarter of all adult women with disabilities (aged 15 years and older) were poor in 1991. Among adult men with disabilities, just over 18 per cent were poor.

Age

There was only a slight variation in poverty rates across age groups for adults with disabilities. The lowest rate of poverty – 19.4 per cent – was among youth aged 15 to 24 with disabilities, many of whom were still living with parents. For other age groups, the poverty rate was fairly consistent at around 22 per cent (Figure 5.2).

There was more variation in poverty rates among persons without disabilities. For them, poverty rates declined steadily with age, then rose sharply for those 65 and older.

Figure 5.1

Poverty rates for women and men aged 15 and older with and without disabilities, 1991

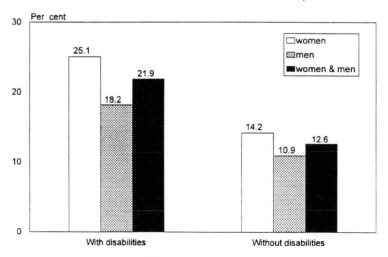

See "Presentation of data" in Chapter 1 for assumptions used.

This steady decline in poverty rates across age groups coincides with increased earnings power during those years, while the rise in rates among those aged 65 and older reflects their withdrawal from the labour force upon retirement.

Figure 5.2

Poverty rates for persons with and without disabilities by age, 1991

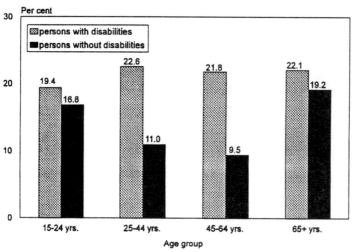

See "Presentation of data" in Chapter 1 for assumptions used.

Severity

Adults with severe disabilities were much more likely to be poor than those with mild disabilities. For adults with mild disabilities, the poverty rate was 17.7 per cent; for those with moderate disabilities, it increased to 23.7 per cent; and among those with severe disabilities, the poverty rate reached a high of 30.3 per cent – nearly one-third (Figure 5.3). Given the labour force disadvantages faced by those with severe disabilities, this high rate is not surprising.[5]

Between 1986 and 1991, poverty rates for those with mild and moderate disabilities decreased. In 1986, 23.1 per

5. Differences in poverty rates by severity level were not due simply to differences in employment, however. When looking only at those who were employed, persons with mild disabilities were still less likely to be poor than those with moderate or severe disabilities.

cent of adults with mild disabilities were poor; in 1991, this rate had dropped to 17.7 per cent. Similarly, the poverty rate among adults with moderate disabilities decreased from 26.9 per cent in 1986 to 23.7 per cent in 1991. Among adults with severe disabilities, however, the percentage who were poor increased slightly during the same period. In 1986, 28.3 per cent of adults with severe disabilities were poor; by 1991, this had risen to 30.3 per cent. There appears to be increasing polarization of poverty rates among persons with disabilities based on the severity of the disability (not illustrated).

The increased labour force participation of persons with mild disabilities that occurred between 1986 and 1991 (discussed in Chapter 2), no doubt, contributed to their reduced rate of poverty. And while persons with severe disabilities also increased their labour force participation during that period, they were much less successful in actually getting jobs. This may help to explain the slight increase in poverty among this group.

Figure 5.3

Poverty rates for persons aged 15 and older with disabilities by severity of disability, 1991

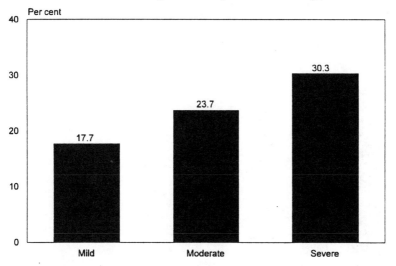

See "Presentation of data" in Chapter 1 for assumptions used.

Type of disability

In Chapters 2 and 3, it was evident that those with hearing and unknown physical disabilities were the least disadvantaged in the labour force. Adults with either of these two disability types also had the lowest poverty rates in 1991. Among persons with hearing disabilities, the poverty rate was 20.2 per cent; for those with unknown physical disabilities, the rate was lowest at 16.2 per cent (Figure 5.4). Those with speaking disabilities were almost twice as likely to be poor (31.2 per cent). Persons with seeing disabilities and those with mental/learning disabilities were close behind with rates of 29.6 per cent and 26.8 per cent, respectively.

Living arrangements

In Chapter 2 we learned that living in a household with other people seemed to facilitate labour force participation among persons with disabilities. Living in a household with other people also reduced the likelihood that adults with disabilities would be poor. Among adults with disabilities who lived in a household with other people, the poverty rate in 1991 was 16.5 per cent; among those living alone, the

Figure 5.4

Poverty rates for persons aged 15 and older with disabilities by disability type, 1991

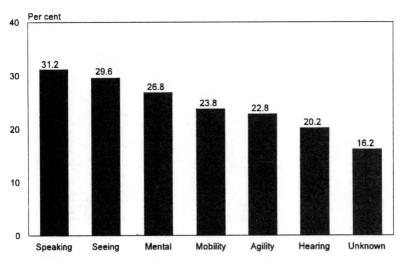

See "Presentation of data" in Chapter 1 for assumptions used.

poverty rate was almost three times higher at 45.5 per cent (Figure 5.5). Women with disabilities were most disadvantaged by living alone – nearly half of those who lived alone lived in poverty.

Living alone is likely to increase poverty rates among persons with disabilities for two important reasons. First, as previously discussed, persons with disabilities who live alone are less likely to have a job and to have earnings than those who live with others. And as discussed later, those with earnings are less likely to be poor. Second, for those who live with others, it is possible to have more than one income coming into the household; those who live alone must rely upon only one income.

Figure 5.5

Poverty rates for women and men aged 15 and older with disabilities by living arrangements, 1991

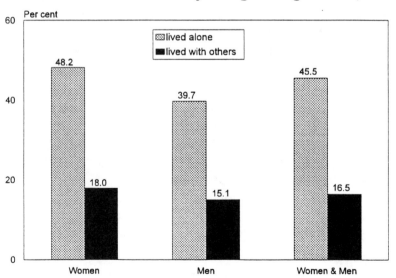

See "Presentation of data" in Chapter 1 for assumptions used.

Urban versus rural residence

Poverty among adults with disabilities living in rural areas is lower than among those living in urban settings. For those in rural areas, 16.1 per cent were poor in 1991; for those in urban areas, the rate was 23.6 per cent (not shown).

At least four factors – sex, severity, labour force status and living arrangements – help explain these differences in urban/rural poverty rates among persons with disabilities. Adults with disabilities who lived in rural areas were more likely to be men, to have a mild disability, to be employed and to live with others – all characteristics associated with lower rates of poverty.[6] When, for example, only employed men with mild disabilities and shared living arrangements are compared, the differences in urban/rural poverty rates disappear almost entirely (not shown).

Level of education[7]

As already discussed, higher levels of education are associated with greater labour force participation, better employment prospects and higher levels of earnings. It is not surprising, therefore, that higher levels of education are also associated with lower rates of poverty (Figure 5.6). This holds true for both those with and without disabilities. Among persons with disabilities, 28.3 per cent of those who had not completed high school were poor, compared to 13.4 per cent for those with post-secondary education. Among persons without disabilities, the comparable poverty rates were 16.2 per cent and 8 per cent, respectively.

Among persons with disabilities, poverty rates for those who had not completed high school were more than double the rates for persons with post-secondary education. But even those with post-secondary education were still more likely to be poor than their counterparts without disabilities.

---

6. Of these four factors, labour force status appears to have had the greatest impact on poverty rate differences between those living in urban and rural areas.

7. In the HALS, highest level of education was available only for those aged 15 to 64.

In fact, the ratio of poverty rates among persons with disabilities compared to those for persons without disabilities is roughly similar at each level of education attained. And while the likelihood of living in poverty goes down for both groups as their level of education increases, the gap between those with and those without disabilities remains.

Figure 5.6

Poverty rates for persons with and without disabilities by highest level of education, 1991

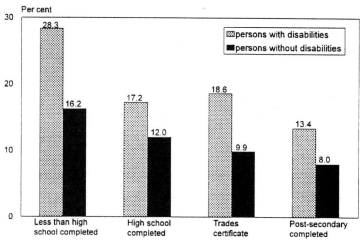

See "Presentation of data" in Chapter 1 for assumptions used.

Labour force status

Labour force status is one of the most important factors in determining whether an adult with a disability is likely to be poor. Adults with disabilities who were employed were much less likely to be poor than those who were either unemployed or out of the labour force altogether. Employed persons with disabilities had a poverty rate of 13.4 per cent, compared to 23.9 per cent for their unemployed counterparts and 31 per cent for those who were out of the labour force. Seniors (aged 65 and older) with disabilities had a poverty rate of 22.1 per cent (Figure 5.7).

A similar pattern was found among persons without disabilities, but again, they were less likely to be poor than those with disabilities in each instance.

Figure 5.7

Poverty rates for persons aged 15 and older with and without disabilities by labour force status, 1991

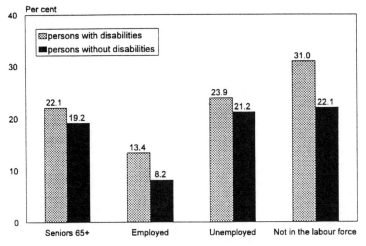

See "Presentation of data" in Chapter 1 for assumptions used.

Figure 5.8

Poverty rates for persons aged 15 and older with disabilities by cause of disability, 1991

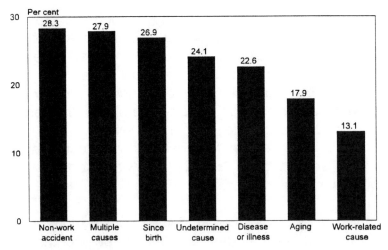

See "Presentation of data" in Chapter 1 for assumptions used.

Cause of the disability

The underlying condition that caused a disability had a notable effect on poverty rates. Those with disabilities stemming from non-work accidents had the highest poverty rate in 1991 at 28.3 per cent (Figure 5.8). They were closely followed by those whose disability resulted from multiple causes (27.9 per cent), and those who were born with the condition (26.9 per cent). The lowest poverty rate was among those with disabilities resulting from work-related causes – either due to accidents or environmental factors – at 13.1 per cent. Persons with a disability caused by aging had the second lowest rate at 17.9 per cent.

These patterns can be explained, in part, by other factors that also affect poverty rates. For example, those with work-related causes were less likely to have severe disabilities, less likely to live alone, more likely to be employed and more likely, by far, to be men. As we have already seen, all of these characteristics were associated with lower poverty rates.

The high rate of poverty among persons with disabilities from multiple causes reflects the fact that such disabilities were more likely to be severe, and that these individuals were more likely to live alone and to be out of the labour force – all factors associated with higher poverty rates.

However, factors such as severity, sex, living arrangements and labour force status did not account for all of the differences in poverty rates. Other factors came into play here, one of the most significant being the source of income for those who could not rely on earnings. For example, those who were out of the labour force and had a disability from a work-related cause were more likely to have access to support from such programs as Workers' Compensation. And although Workers' Compensation provides higher levels of financial support than programs like social assistance, it is available only to those with disabilities resulting from work-related causes.

Income sources for persons with disabilities[8]

While previous chapters have focussed on labour force issues and earnings of persons with disabilities, there are non-market sources of income that must be mentioned as well. In this section, a brief overview of the income support system for persons with disabilities is presented. The overview is brief because there are other information sources which have dealt with these issues in depth. The object of this review is merely to acquaint the reader with the variety of sources of income support available.

Canada's disability income support system

The disability income support system in Canada has been described as a "patch-work collection of programs."[9] The level of support actually provided to persons with disabilities can vary significantly, depending on the program for which an individual is eligible. Cause of disability and participation in the paid labour force are two of the most important factors that determine program eligibility for adults.[10]

---

8. Additional information on sources of income for persons with disabilities at the provincial and Census Metropolitan Area levels, based on 1991 Census data, is available from the Canadian Clearinghouse on Disability Issues, Office for Disability Issues, Human Resources Development Canada (Tel: 1-800-665-9017 or TTY 1-800-561-9706). There are, however, some differences in the methods used to identify a disability between the Census and the HALS (and the LMAS).

9. See Muszynski, 1990, p. 32. Canada is not unique in the world with respect to the fragmentation of income support systems for persons with disabilities. And, as in some other countries, various proposals over the years have sought to streamline the system. For a discussion about such proposals and the income support system, see: Ison, 1994; Muszynski, 1990; Federal/Provincial/Territorial Review, 1993; Ontario Ministry of Community and Social Services, 1988; and The Roeher Institute, 1988, 1992, 1993b and 1993c. For a discussion of the housing system available to persons with disabilities in Canada, see The Roeher Institute, 1990.

10. Benefits for children with disabilities constitute a different stream of programs.

In 1991, nearly one-quarter of adults with disabilities received income from some program as a result of their disability. The remainder relied on earnings, retirement pensions not related to the disability, or they received full or partial economic support from their family and friends.

Income support programs for persons with disabilities can be organized into three main streams: insurance programs, non-insurance income support and the tort system.

1. Insurance Programs

These are aimed at income replacement for working-age persons with disabilities who have participated in the labour force. Among these programs are: CPP/QPP disability benefits, Workers' Compensation (provincially based), Unemployment Insurance sickness benefits (for short-term disabilities) and a variety of private insurance schemes. Eligibility for these programs is dependent on the individual's past labour force participation, the cause of the disability and the extent of the disability.

CPP/QPP disability benefits, for example, are dependent on both past labour force participation and the extent of the disability. These benefits are available to persons under the age of 65 who have been in the paid labour force and contributed to the Plan for a certain period of time.[11] To qualify for benefits under CPP/QPP, a disability must be both "severe and prolonged." A severe disability is one that renders an individual incapable of "regularly pursuing any substantially gainful occupation." A prolonged disability is one that is expected to last for a significant period of time (the duration of which cannot be determined) or until death.

---

11. At present, individuals become eligible for benefits after contributing for two of the previous three years, or five of the last 10 years.

CPP/QPP disability benefits are terminated if the recipient ceases to have a disability and is once again capable of "regularly pursuing gainful employment," upon death, or when they reach the age of 65 and are automatically switched to a CPP/QPP retirement pension. Individuals who lack sufficient labour force experience are excluded from this program. Those who acquire a disability early in life and women who have been out of the labour force due to domestic responsibilities are the most likely to lack such experience and thus be excluded from these benefits.

The eligibility requirements for CPP/QPP are further complicated by the fact that there can be a tremendous amount of flux in both the severity and existence of a disability from year to year, as noted in the previous chapter. In the past, these eligibility requirements presented difficulties for those with cyclical disabilities. In attempting to find employment during periods when work was possible, such individuals risked the financial security that these benefits provided. When their disability recurred or increased in severity, they again faced a four-month waiting period and the difficult application procedure to reapply for the benefits. Fortunately, in late 1995, Human Resources Development Canada established a number of measures to remove some of these barriers for CPP recipients. Among the measures is a specific provision for those with cyclical or degenerative disabilities to be "reinstated on a fast-track basis if the disability recurs."

Eligibility for programs such as Workers' Compensation is dependent on labour force participation and cause of disability. These provincial programs provide benefits only to those who acquire their disability as a result of an on-the-job injury or industrial disease. Among working-age persons with disabilities in 1991, only about 22 per cent acquired their disability in such a manner. However, Workers' Compensation benefits are usually more generous than those offered under other programs. As noted previously, adults who acquired a disability as a result of a work-related cause were less likely to be poor than those who acquired a disability from any other cause. This is not surprising since they were also more likely to collect Workers' Compensation.

Regarding cause of disability, there is considerable variation according to sex. Approximately 34 per cent of working-age men with disabilities acquired their disability through job-related accidents or illnesses, compared to only about 11 per cent for their female counterparts. This means that women are much less likely than men to qualify for Workers' Compensation benefits. (While CPP/QPP disability benefits are available only to those with the most severe disabilities, Workers' Compensation can provide partial benefits for less severe disabilities.)

Automobile insurance schemes can also provide support for those who acquire a disability as a result of an automobile accident. However, only a small proportion of all persons with disabilities derive income support from such schemes.

2.   **Non-insurance Income Support**
For people who are ineligible for income support from the insurance programs mentioned above, social assistance or welfare becomes the main alternative source for income security. In some provinces, and under certain circumstances, persons with disabilities may get higher levels of support from social assistance than those without disabilities. Typically these higher levels of support are contingent upon the individual being designated as "unemployable." (As we saw previously, however, designating an individual with a disability as "unemployable" may not be appropriate, given the

fact that for many people, disability is not a static state, and one's employability depends on both the nature of the disability and the surrounding environment.) Designating individuals as unemployable can discourage them from seeking employment during those periods when their disability or environmental conditions permit.

In many provinces, supports and services such as subsidies for assistive devices, medications, transportation and home care can be provided to individuals as long as they are eligible for social assistance. For these individuals, entry into the paid labour market can mean the loss of income security as well as the loss of these important supports and services. Unless they are able to find secure employment that will generate sufficient earnings to cover their basic living expenses plus the extra costs of the needed services, entering the paid labour market could leave them significantly worse off.

3.   The Tort System

For persons who acquire their disability as a result of an accident caused by someone else's negligence, the courts provide another source of income security in the form of tort liability. While some of these awards can be quite generous, this system applies to only a relatively small proportion of all persons with disabilities. In addition to restricting these awards to those with a disability caused by the negligence of another, they cannot be sought in cases where the right to sue is precluded. For example, Workers' Compensation removes the right to sue for workplace accidents and some provincial automobile insurance plans do the same for road accidents.

Income source and poverty

While having a disability increases the odds that a person will live in poverty, the odds are not equal for all those with disabilities. The disability support system in Canada "has been likened to a lottery."[12] The proportion of persons with disabilities living below Statistics Canada's low income cut-offs varies considerably, depending on whether a person's livelihood is derived from earnings, from one of the income support programs, or through support from family or friends. As mentioned, persons with disabilities who were employed had a poverty rate of 13.4 per cent. Almost 28 per cent of those receiving CPP/QPP disability benefits were poor; 14.5 per cent of those receiving Workers' Compensation were poor; and 64.1 per cent of those on social assistance were poor (Figure 5.9).

Persons with disabilities who must rely on social assistance for their income support have by far the greatest likelihood of living in poverty. Those with employment earnings and those on Workers' Compensation are the least

Figure 5.9

Poverty rates for persons with disabilities who received disability income from CPP/QPP Disability, Workers' Compensation or Social Assistance, 1991

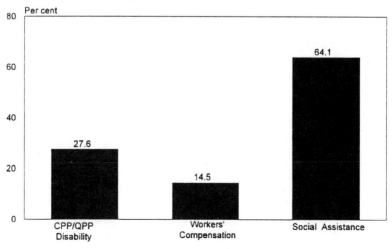

See "Presentation of data" in Chapter 1 for assumptions used.

12. Ontario Ministry of Community and Social Services, 1988, p. 106.

likely to be poor. Among those who had neither earnings nor disability income support, 23.6 per cent were poor. This group includes those who were supported by family or friends (particularly in the case of those aged 15 to 64), as well as those who had non-disability related pensions (particularly in the case of those aged 65 and older).

Sources of income for persons with disabilities

About 12 per cent of adults (under the age of 65) with disabilities had no personal income from either earnings, disability income support programs, or from investments. Presumably, these individuals received their economic support from family or friends. The remaining 88 per cent had some income from one or more of these three sources (earnings, disability income support programs or investments). Nearly 11 per cent of this population collected some social assistance benefits, about 10 per cent collected CPP/QPP disability benefits, and about 6 per cent collected Workers' Compensation. In total, about 30 per cent collected some form of disability-related income and about 61 per cent had some earnings.

Income sources of those aged 65 and older are more difficult to determine from the HALS. Some may have had earnings, but the HALS does not contain earnings information for persons over the age of 64. It is possible, however, to determine that almost all of those over age 64 with disabilities had some personal income and only 14 per cent had income from a disability-related source. The majority of these individuals would have derived income from retirement pension plans, both public and private.

Discussion

Having a disability increases a person's chances of being poor. Adults with disabilities derive their economic support from a variety of sources and their chances of being poor vary, depending on the source of that income support. Those who receive income from labour force earnings are least likely to be poor; for those who must rely on an income support program, their odds of living in poverty can vary widely, depending on the program.

The two most important factors which determine eligibility for a disability income program are an individual's past labour force participation and how the disability occurred. Persons who have sufficient labour force involvement can qualify for such programs as CPP/QPP disability benefits, private disability pensions, or Workers' Compensation. These are considered as income replacement programs and they provide benefits that are likely to be more generous than those available under social assistance. Social assistance is the only other alternative source of income available to individuals who lack sufficient labour force experience.[13]

The most generous programs of all are provincially based Workers' Compensation programs, which are available only to those who acquire a disability as a direct result of a work-related accident or industrial illness. For people who have no earnings, do not qualify for income replacement because of a lack of labour force participation, and who cannot rely on family and friends for financial support, social assistance becomes the most likely source of income support. It is this latter group of individuals who face the greatest likelihood of living in poverty – in 1991, nearly two-thirds of adults with disabilities who were on social assistance were poor.

---

13. Of course, a small proportion of individuals who acquired a disability through non-work-related injuries may have access to benefits through automobile insurance plans or through legal action under tort liability.

About 12 per cent of persons between the ages of 15 and 64 with disabilities had no personal income from either earnings, pensions, disability income support programs, investments or other sources. Presumably, these individuals had to rely on financial support from family or friends. About one-quarter of those with no personal income were living with their parents and most were students. Nearly two-thirds of those without personal income were living with spouses (more than half of these were women with children living at home). About one in 10 individuals without personal income were living outside family situations, either alone or with non-family members.

The poverty rates used here are based on family income and are adjusted for family size and the size of the community. However, they are not adjusted for the extra costs involved in having a disability. Even beyond the costs of foregone earnings opportunities, persons with disabilities must often spend additional money for items and services related to their disability. Such expenditures can include medication, special transportation, medical services not

Figure 5.10

Non-reimbursed out-of-pocket disability-related expenses for persons aged 15 and older with disabilities, 1991

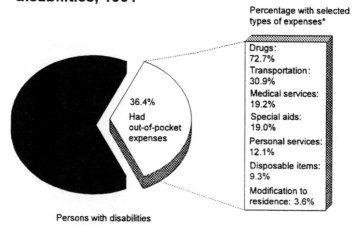

Percentage with selected types of expenses*

Drugs: 72.7%
Transportation: 30.9%
Medical services: 19.2%
Special aids: 19.0%
Personal services: 12.1%
Disposable items: 9.3%
Modification to residence: 3.6%

36.4%
Had out-of-pocket expenses

Persons with disabilities

*Many individuals had more than one type of expense.
See "Presentation of data" in Chapter 1 for assumptions used.

covered by provincial health care plans, special aids and
assistive devices, and modifications to one's residence. In
1991, 36.4 per cent of adults with disabilities reported
having at least one expenditure related to their disability that
was not reimbursed and for which they were out-of-pocket
(Figure 5.10).[14] For individuals living on very low incomes, it
may come down to a choice between purchasing these
needed items or services and providing other necessities of
life. In some cases, expenditures on these items may also
mean the difference between being able to find a job or not.
Without special aids, special transportation and other
supports and services, some persons with disabilities may
be unable to look for work, disadvantaged in competing for
work, or unable to perform the work.[15] Poverty for those with
special needs can become a trap.

This trap is best exemplified by social assistance
programs that link supports and services to income support
for persons with disabilities. Under such programs,
assistance for required supports is available, but in order to
acquire this assistance, persons with disabilities must often
"trade a valued status (employable) for an unvalued status
(unemployable)."[16] For this reason, proposals have been
made to establish a program of supports and services for
persons with disabilities which is not linked to the welfare

---

14. Many individuals had expenditures for more than one type of item.
15. In addition to keeping a person with a disability from full economic
    participation, poverty can also present a barrier to participating in
    society as an equal citizen. Poverty also renders persons with
    disabilities more vulnerable to abusive and violent situations. For a
    discussion of the relationship between poverty and abuse of persons
    with disabilities, see The Roeher Institute, 1995b.
16. The Roeher Institute, 1993a, p. viii.

system.[17] One of the most noteworthy proposals has come from The Roeher Institute:

> The system would not be a basic income support program. Instead, disability-related policy and programs would be removed entirely from a welfare framework. This would give an alternative to the many people with disabilities who have no option but to apply for welfare in order to qualify for essential disability supports. ...such individuals would be able to qualify for the attendant services, personal support workers, wheelchairs and other supports they require without program criteria that deny them access to the labour force, adult training, educational upgrading and other social and economic opportunities that are available to the non-disabled public.[18]

Throughout this book, it has been noted that women with disabilities appear to be more disadvantaged than men with disabilities in terms of their success in the labour force and their greater likelihood of being poor. The next chapter provides additional details about some of the important economic differences between women and men with disabilities.

---

17. For a thorough discussion of the proposal by the Roeher Institute, see *The Canadian Disability Resource Program: Offsetting Costs of Disability and Assuring Access to Disability-Related Supports* (The Roeher Institute,1994); and *Direct Dollars: A Study of Individualized Funding in Canada* (The Roeher Institute, 1993). For an examination of the present costs of providing supports and services to persons with disabilities in selected provinces, see *Disability-Related Supports: Costs and Delivery System for Selected Provinces* (The Roeher Institute, 1995).

18. The Roeher Institute, 1994, p. 6.

Chapter 6

Women with disabilities:
Progress in the labour market and the domestic labour challenge

Throughout this book, numerous examples have been given of the economic disadvantage faced by women with disabilities. Compared to their male counterparts, women with disabilities have lower rates of participation in the labour force, higher rates of unemployment when they are in the labour force, lower employment earnings, less access to the more generous income support programs, and higher rates of poverty overall.

In spite of all this, however, there are some indications that younger women with disabilities may be improving their economic position relative to their male counterparts. Post-secondary education has been instrumental in narrowing the gender gap in the labour market among persons with disabilities, and this is most evident among the youngest age groups. It is unclear, however, what will happen to these young women as they begin to form families and face the added challenge of increased domestic labour. As in the general population, women with disabilities assume a disproportionate share of domestic labour within their families, and this can have an impact on their labour force participation.

In the first part of this chapter, the recent increase in labour force participation among women with disabilities is reviewed. The second section details the potential contribution of education to this increase, and in the third, the interaction of domestic labour, disability, labour force participation and sex is explored.

Joining the labour force: narrowing the sex gap

While women with disabilities were less likely than their male counterparts to participate in the paid labour force in 1991, they did manage to narrow the sex gap in participation rates from what it had been in 1986. This narrowing effect was due to the fact that women with disabilities increased their labour force participation rate at a much faster pace than the men. Between 1986 and 1991, working-age men with disabilities increased their labour force participation rate – the percentage either employed or unemployed – by eight per cent. During that same period, their female counterparts experienced a 29 per cent increase in their participation rate. The sex gap in participation rates was narrowest among the youngest age groups. Among persons aged 15 to 24 with disabilities, for example, the participation rate for women in 1991 was 96.1 per cent that of their male counterparts. The sex gap increased steadily in each successive age group, ending with women aged 55 to 64 with disabilities whose participation rate was only 47.4 per cent that of the men.[1]

---

1.   In 1991, the participation rate for women with disabilities as a percentage of that for men with disabilities by age group was as follows: aged 15 to 24, 96.1 per cent; aged 25 to 44, 81.4 per cent; aged 45 to 54, 74.3 per cent; and aged 55 to 65, 47.4 per cent (see Figure 2.4 in Chapter 2).

Why do younger women with disabilities have labour force participation rates so much closer to those of their male counterparts than do older women? There are a number of possible explanations. For one thing, younger women with disabilities seem to be increasing their levels of education at a faster pace than men with disabilities, and this may be partly responsible for the narrowing of the sex gap in participation rates. However, this pattern may also reflect the impact of the domestic labour challenge on the labour force participation rates of women with disabilities over their life cycle.

Higher levels of education

From the data presented in Chapter 2, it was clear that higher levels of education attained by persons with disabilities led to greater participation in the labour force. The narrowing of the sex gap in participation rates among younger age groups could be related, at least in part, to the gains in education made by younger women.

Post-secondary education helps narrow the sex gap

Post-secondary education is particularly important for women with disabilities, and it can be a significant factor in narrowing the participation gap with their male counterparts. In 1991, the sex gap in labour force participation rates among persons with disabilities was considerably narrower for those with post-secondary education, both university and non-university (Figure 6.1). Among persons with disabilities whose highest level of education was primary school or less, the participation rate for women was about 53 per cent that of men (25.3 per cent participation rate for women, compared to 48.2 per cent participation rate for men). Women's participation rates as a proportion of men's rose to about 92 per cent for those with either a non-university post-secondary diploma (67.5 per cent participation rate for women, compared to 73.4 per cent participation rate for men) or a university degree (69.8 per cent participation rate for women, compared to 76 per cent participation rate for men). So, while a higher level of educational attainment was important in the labour force participation rates of both sexes, it had a stronger impact on women with disabilities than on their male counterparts – and thus, had a narrowing effect on the sex gap in participation.

Figure 6.1

Labour force participation rates* of women and men with disabilities by highest level of education, 1991

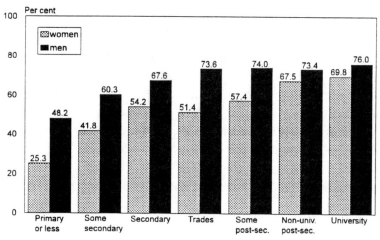

*employed or unemployed
See "Presentation of data" in Chapter 1 for assumptions used.

Younger women step up the pace

There is also evidence that younger women with disabilities may be helping to narrow the sex gap in labour force participation rates by increasing their level of educational attainment at a faster pace than young men with disabilities.

Among persons aged 45 to 64 with disabilities, 13.2 per cent of the men in 1991 had post-secondary education, compared to 16.2 per cent of the women (Figure 6.2). For the next youngest group – those aged 25 to 44 – the rate of post-secondary school completion was higher for both sexes. This reflects a similar trend in the general population toward increasing numbers of younger people completing post-secondary education. Nevertheless, the relative difference between women and men in these two age groups was similar – women aged 45 to 64 were 1.2 times more likely than their male counterparts to have completed post-secondary education, and for those aged 25 to 44, the figure was 1.3. However, among those aged 15 to 24, women with disabilities were 2.4 times more likely to have completed post-secondary education than men. Of these young women, 10.7 per cent had post-secondary education, compared to 4.5 per cent of the men.[2]

This suggests that among the youngest group of persons with disabilities, women were increasing their educational attainment at a much faster pace than men.

Figure 6.2

Percentage of women and men with disabilities with post-secondary education, by age, 1991

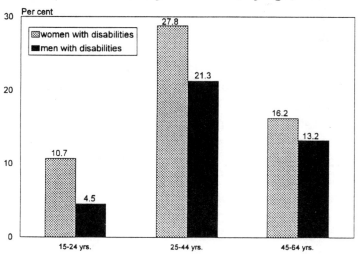

See "Presentation of data" in Chapter 1 for assumptions used.

2. Among persons without disabilities, a similar age trend was found, although the sex difference among the youngest age group was not as pronounced as it was among persons with disabilities. Also, men aged 45 to 64 without disabilities had a slightly higher likelihood of having post-secondary education than their female counterparts.

Of course, the percentage of either sex aged 15 to 24 with completed post-secondary credentials seems rather low compared to the group aged 25 to 44. This is because many in the youngest age group were still pursuing their education and had not yet reached an age where post-secondary graduation was possible. It is impossible to determine whether the trend just noted would still be evident once all the young people had a chance to finish their education; however, there are indications that the trend might well continue. In 1991, younger women (aged 15-24) with disabilities were more likely than their male counterparts to be pursuing their education, thus making them more likely to ultimately obtain post-secondary credentials. About 62 per cent of young women with disabilities were still enrolled in school in 1991, compared to 56 per cent of their male counterparts.[3]

The increasing proportion of younger women attaining post-secondary credentials reflects what has happened in the general population. With the resurgence of the women's movement in the 1960s and 1970s, greater numbers of women in general obtained post-secondary education.[4] Women with disabilities were no exception to this trend; in fact, the trend may have been even stronger among women who acquired their disability at a young age. As noted in Chapter 2, there is evidence that those who knew about their disability before they completed their schooling were likely to have higher rates of labour force participation than those who acquired a disability after completing their education. One possible explanation for this finding is that these individuals may have been better able to plan their education to suit the labour force challenges they would face as a result of their disability. School-aged women with disabilities, therefore, may be even more aware of the

---

3. As discussed in Chapter 2, the participation rate for women aged 15 to 24 who were not in school was actually higher than that for men.
4. While an increasing proportion of men also pursued post-secondary education during this same period, the increase among women was greater.

benefits of higher education than school-aged women without disabilities.

It is difficult to determine whether these young women represent a unique group in history – women with disabilities who may be better informed about the economic challenges of life as a woman with a disability and, therefore, better able to prepare for these challenges than previous groups.[5]

There is also no way of knowing how this youngest group of women will deal with the challenges of domestic labour within a family situation, since the vast majority have yet to form families of their own. About 80 per cent of women aged 15 to 24 – with and without disabilities – were single in 1991. While most of these women lived with parents,[6] their role in the family with respect to the division of domestic labour was probably quite different from the role they would assume once they were out on their own or had formed their own families.

The domestic labour challenge

Similar to women in the general population, the labour force participation of women with disabilities is affected by childbearing, childrearing and other domestic responsibilities. Historically, women have delayed, interrupted or foregone careers in the paid labour market to stay at home with their children and provide domestic labour such as housework, grocery shopping, laundry, meal preparation, and so on. The situation is no different for women with disabilities. In this section, labour force participation and economic security are examined in light of the impact of dependent children, marital status, and the performance of household chores.

---

5. The economic future of women with disabilities depends not only on the trends among very young women with disabilities, but also on the trends among very young women without disabilities.
6. In 1991, over two-thirds of women aged 15 to 24 with disabilities were still living with one or both parents.

The impact of dependent children

Preschool-aged children have a decided impact on the labour force participation of women with and without disabilities. In 1991, the vast majority of women with children under the age of six were in the 25 to 44 age group. For that reason, the data presented in this section focuses on this age group and on the two 10-year age groups within it (that is, those aged 25 to 34 and those aged 35 to 44).

Women with disabilities who had children under the age of six were less likely to be in the paid labour force than those who had no dependent children or had school-aged children. Among women aged 25 to 34 with disabilities, for example, 68.2 per cent of those who had no dependent children were in the paid labour force; for those with children under age six, the figure dipped to 59.8 per cent, and for those with children over age five, it was 62.9 per cent (Figure 6.3).

Figure 6.3

Labour force participation rates* of women aged 25-34 , with and without disabilities, by presence of dependent children, 1991

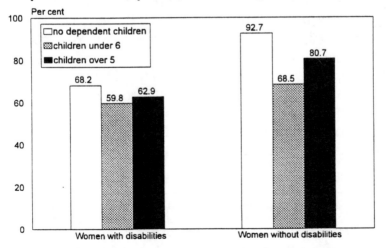

*employed or unemployed
See "Presentation of data" in Chapter 1 for assumptions used.

A similar, but more pronounced, pattern was found among women aged 25 to 34 without disabilities. Women in this group who had no children had the highest participation rate, and those with preschool-aged children had the lowest participation rate, suggesting that many women may be out of the paid labour force while engaged in childrearing. The participation rate for women with school-aged children rebounds somewhat, suggesting that some women may enter, or re-enter, the paid labour force once their children are in school.

As illustrated in Figure 6.4, this pattern also held true for women without disabilities who were slightly older (aged 35 to 44). However, among women aged 35 to 44 with disabilities, there was little difference in the labour force participation of those without children and those with children under six years of age. This can be explained, in part, by the fact that women aged 35 to 44 with disabilites who had no children were also much more likely to have had

Figure 6.4

Labour force participation rates* of women aged 35-44 , with and without disabilities, by presence of dependent children, 1991

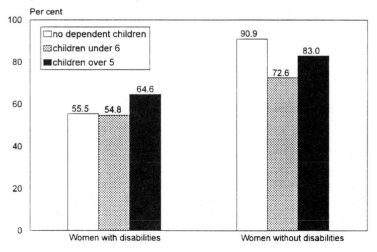

*employed or unemployed
See "Presentation of data" in Chapter 1 for assumptions used.

severe disabilities than either women aged 25 to 34 without children or those aged 35 to 44 with children.

As seen in Chapter 2, those with more severe disabilities were less likely to participate in the paid labour market. Women with more severe disabilities were also less likely to ever have had children; and the difference in fertility patterns between women with mild disabilities and those with severe disabilities was most pronounced among the older age groups, beginning with those aged 35 to 44 (Figure 6.5). The increased severity of the disabilities among women aged 35 to 44 without dependent children, therefore, was a factor in both their lower participation rates and their unlikelihood of ever having had children.

Overall, the presence of preschool-aged children had a negative impact on the participation rates of their mothers, but this trend only became evident when women older than 24 were examined. Women aged 15 to 24 with disabilities had not yet experienced the negative impact of this trend

Figure 6.5

Proportion of women with mild and severe disabilities who never had children*, by age, 1991

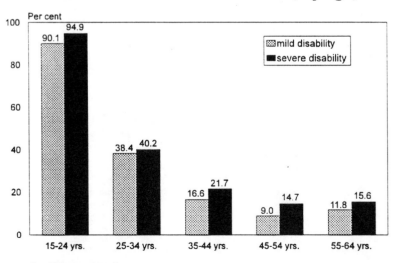

*no children ever born alive
See "Presentation of data" in Chapter 1 for assumptions used.

due to their relatively low fertility rates. An important question (which, unfortunately, cannot be answered by these data) is: Would these young women with disabilities, who seemed to be closing the gap in participation rates with men, follow the same path as the older women once they entered the family-formation stage of their life cycle?

The economic impact of dependent children under the age of six can also be seen in the experiences of the women who were employed. In 1991, about 12 per cent of all employed women aged 15 to 64 with disabilities who either had no dependent children or dependent children over the age of five reported that they required some form of job redesign to continue working. Among their counterparts with children under the age of six, this figure was higher at about 19 per cent (not illustrated). This suggests that their requirements for job redesign may not have been due solely to their disability, but rather to the interaction of their disability with their domestic responsibilities.

Having to make changes to one's work seems to have a greater impact on the economic well-being of women with disabilities than it does on men with disabilities. The poverty rates of women who made changes to the kind or amount of work they did, or changed the actual job they did, were higher than the poverty rates of women who had not made such changes. However, there was very little difference in the poverty rates of men with disabilities, regardless of whether they had made such changes. Figure 6.6 illustrates the poverty rates in 1991 for women and men with disabilities who changed the kind of work they performed in order to accommodate their disability.[7] The poverty rate among employed adult men (aged 15 to 64) with disabilities was fairly constant at around 12 per cent, regardless of whether or not they had changed the kind of work they performed. For women, however, making such a change

---

7. An almost identical pattern was found for those who changed the amount of work they performed and for those who had changed jobs altogether.

resulted in a higher rate of poverty (20.5 per cent, compared to14.4 per cent).

As indicated earlier, women with preschool-aged children were more likely to require some form of job redesign in order to continue working. Yet, making changes at work to accommodate a disability had a much more negative impact on the economic circumstances of women with disabilities (an increased likelihood of poverty) than it did on their male counterparts. Employed women with disabilities who had preschool-aged children were more likely to require some form of job redesign and, unfortunately, this made them more likely to live in poverty.

Figure 6.6

Poverty rates of employed women and men with disabilities by whether they changed the kind of work they performed, 1991

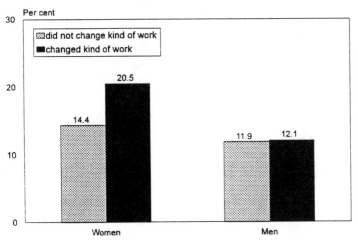

See "Presentation of data" in Chapter 1 for assumptions used.

Marital status

Women with disabilities were more likely than those without disabilities to be lone parents of dependent children.[8] About 8 per cent of women aged 25 to 44 without disabilities were lone parents in 1991; the rate of lone parenthood among women with disabilities, however, was almost twice this at 16 per cent (not illustrated). The participation rate of women with disabilities who were lone parents was lower than that of their counterparts in two-parent families. For example, in 1991, the participation rate for those who were lone parents of preschool-aged children was 62.8 per cent; the rate for those in two-parent families was 70.2 per cent (not illustrated).[9] The greater likelihood of being a lone parent, coupled with lower participation rates among lone parents, contributed to the lower likelihood of labour force participation among women with disabilities.

Figure 6.7
Marital status* of women and men aged 25-44 with and without disabilities, 1991

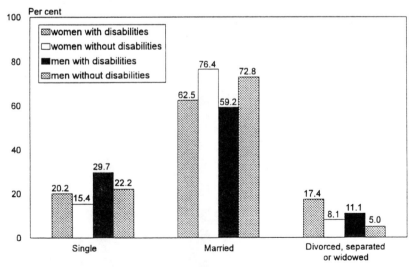

* Common-law partners are included under married category.
See "Presentation of data" in Chapter 1 for assumptions used.

8. The rate of lone parenthood among men with disabilities (about 3 per cent) was much lower than that of women with disabilities.
9. A similar pattern was found among women without disabilities.

One of the primary reasons why women with disabilities were more likely to be lone parents than women without disabilities was their greater likelihood of being divorced, separated or widowed.[10] As illustrated in Figure 6.7, 17.4 per cent of women aged 25 to 44 with disabilities were divorced, separated or widowed; among women of that age without disabilities, less than half this percentage (8.1 per cent) were in the same situation. Women with disabilities were also more likely to be single than women without disabilities (20.2 per cent, compared to 15.4 per cent), but that was not the main reason for higher rates of lone parenthood. About 78 per cent of women aged 25 to 44 with disabilities who were lone parents were divorced, separated or widowed; for those without disabilities, the figure was 71 per cent (not illustrated).

The greater tendency for women with disabilities to become divorced, separated or widowed was evident in

Figure 6.8

Marital status* of women and men <u>aged 45-64</u> with and without disabilities, 1991

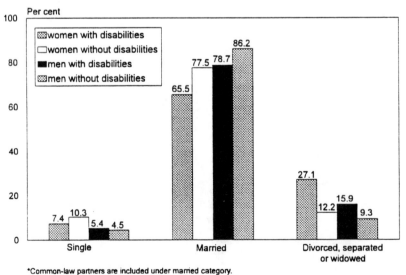

*Common-law partners are included under married category.
See "Presentation of data" in Chapter 1 for assumptions used.

10.   It is impossible to distinguish between divorce, separation and widowhood using the HALS.

other age groups as well. For example, among women aged 45 to 64 with disabilities, 27.1 per cent were divorced, separated or widowed (Figure 6.8). For women without disabilities, less than half that percentage were in the same situation (12.2 per cent). As illustrated in Figures 6.7 and 6.8, women with disabilities were also more likely than men with disabilities to be divorced, separated or widowed.

Assistance with household chores

In addition to child care, women with disabilities were also more likely than men with disabilities to assume a greater responsibility for basic household chores. Regardless of living arrangements or the severity of their disability, the women were much more likely to perform household chores without assistance. Men with disabilities were much more likely to have assistance with household chores – whether it was required for the disability or not.

The vast majority of both women and men who reported having a disability in 1991 did not require assistance due to their disability for basic household chores such as meal preparation and everyday housework.[11] However, there were some major differences between the sexes concerning those who did receive such assistance. About two-thirds of working-age women with disabilities said they did not have assistance with meal preparation and did not require it as a result of their disability; only about one-quarter of the men reported this (Table 6.1). Nearly two-thirds of working-age men with disabilities said they had assistance with meal preparation, even though they did not require it as a result of their disability; less than one-fifth of their female counterparts were in this position. For assistance with everyday housework, the patterns were similar. As well,

---

11. In 1991, about 85 per cent of women and 89 per cent of men with disabilities (aged 15 to 64) reported that they did not require help with meal preparation as a result of their disability; among seniors, the figures for women and men were 80 per cent and 81 per cent, respectively. Similarly, 73 per cent of women and 87 per cent of men with disabilities (aged 15 to 64) reported that they did not require assistance with everyday housework due to their disability; among seniors, the figures for women and men were 56 per cent and 77 per cent, respectively (See Tables 6.1 and 6.2).

Table 6.1

Women and men aged 15-64 with disabilities: requirements for assistance with meal preparation, 1991

	Women %	Men %
Did not require help because of disability		
Had help with meals	17.7	65.0
Did not have help with meals	66.8	24.3
Total	84.5	89.3
Required help because of disability		
Had sufficient help with meals	7.8	5.7
Had help with meals but needed more help	3.9	4.4
Did not have help with meals but needed help	3.8	0.7
Total	15.5	10.7

See "Presentation of data" in Chapter 1 for assumptions used.

Table 6.2

Women and men aged 65 and older with disabilities: requirements for assistance with meal preparation, 1991

	Women	Men
Did not require help because of disability		
Had help with meals	10.2	63.8
Did not have help with meals	69.3	17.5
Total	79.4	81.3
Required help because of disability		
Had sufficient help with meals	13.0	13.4
Had help with meals but needed more help	5.6	4.0
Did not have help with meals but needed help	1.9	1.3 *
Total	20.6	18.7

* Figure should be used with caution; sample size too low to yield stable estimates.
See "Presentation of data" in Chapter 1 for assumptions used.

much the same trends were found among seniors
(Table 6.2).

So, while the majority of both women and men with
disabilities did not require assistance with basic household
chores strictly because of their disability, the majority of men
were likely to receive assistance anyway; the majority of
women were not. It is clear from Tables 6.1 and 6.2 that
even when assistance with these household chores was
required as a result of the disability, women were more likely
to have their need for assistance unmet.

Assistance with household chores and age

Regardless of their age, the majority of men with
disabilities did not require assistance with meal preparation,
but they received it nonetheless. Between 61.8 and 67.5 per
cent of men with disabilities in each age group were in this
situation, whereas there were greater differences among the
age groups for women with disabilities (Figure 6.9). Within

Figure 6.9

**Percentage of women and men with disabilities who
had assistance with meal preparation but did not
require assistance due to disability, by age, 1991**

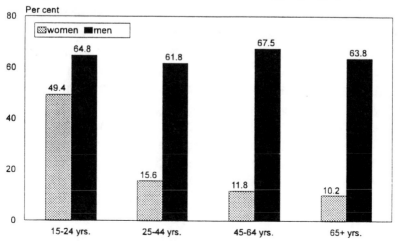

See "Presentation of data" in Chapter 1 for assumptions used.

the three older groups, the percentage of women who did not require assistance but received it anyway was consistently low, from 15.6 per cent (among 25 to 44-year-olds) to 10.2 per cent (among seniors). Among very young women with disabilities, however, 49.4 per cent had assistance with meal preparation, even though they did not require it as a result of their disability. Similar patterns were found when examining assistance with everyday housework.

Again, one wonders whether this youngest group of women (aged 15 to 24) with disabilities is unique in history or simply at a different stage of their life cycle. As they grow older and go out on their own or form their own families, they might continue to get more assistance with domestic chores than their predecessors. It is possible, however, that in 1991 many of these young women had assistance with household chores, despite not requiring it for their disability, simply because most were still living with one or both parents. As a child in a family household, they might not have been required to take full responsibility for meal preparation or everyday housework; as they grow older, however, they may assume the same patterns as were found among the older groups of women.

Assistance with household chores and participation rates

Those who did not need assistance with household chores because of their disability had higher labour force participation rates than those who needed such assistance – regardless of whether or not such assistance was, in fact, received (not illustrated). This was true for both women and men with disabilities. The vast majority of both women and men reported that they did not require assistance with household chores. Those who received assistance anyway were even more likely to be in the paid labour force, and men were much more likely than women to have had such assistance.

Figure 6.10 summarizes the labour force participation rates of working-age women and men with disabilities who did not need assistance with meal preparation as a result of their disability. Among the women who had help with meal preparation, 61.9 per cent were in the paid labour force; among those who did not have assistance with meals, the participation rate was lower, at just over 49 per cent. Similarly, among the men who had help with meal preparation, 72 per cent were in the labour force, compared to 61.9 per cent of those who did not receive help. While these individuals may have reported that their disability did not require them to have assistance with meal preparation, having such assistance was certainly associated with greater participation in the paid labour force. Similar patterns were found for assistance with everyday housework chores.

Figure 6.10

Labour force participation rates* of women and men with disabilities, by having/not having assistance** with meal preparation, 1991

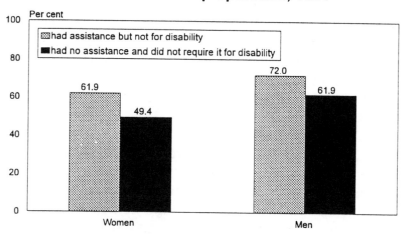

*employed or unemployed
**for those who did not require assistance due to disability
See "Presentation of data" in Chapter 1 for assumptions used.

Living arrangements: who does the chores?

Men were more likely than women to have assistance with household chores. This assistance may have been provided by someone else in the household, a relative or friend outside the household, hired help or through a service agency. It may have involved simply sharing chores with others or having someone else do the task entirely. Logistically, it would seem easier to obtain assistance with everyday household chores if other people were living in the same household. It is likely, therefore, that these patterns of assistance with domestic tasks vary by living arrangements.

Indeed, having assistance with household chores was very much related to whether the individual lived alone or with others. The vast majority of women and men with disabilities who lived alone performed the basic household chores by themselves. However, even among those who lived alone, men were more likely than women to share such chores with others or to have others perform the chores entirely. For example, 93.6 per cent of working-age women who lived alone in 1991 prepared meals by themselves; only 4.2 per cent shared this task with others and a mere 2.2 per cent had someone else prepare their meals entirely (Figure 6.11). Among their male counterparts, 84 per cent prepared meals by themselves, 8.6 per cent shared the task and 7 per cent had someone else prepare their meals. Similar patterns were found among seniors of both sexes who lived alone (Figure 6.12), except that seniors were more likely to share the meal preparation or to have someone else do it for them. This was also evident when examining everyday housework chores (not illustrated).

It was quite a different story, however, for those who lived with other people. The vast majority of women with disabilities who lived with others performed their own meal preparation – 69 per cent of working-age women and 65.9 per cent of senior women (Figures 6.11 and 6.12). For men with disabilities who lived with others, the situation was completely reversed; they were most likely to have had someone else prepare their meals for them – 46.6 per cent of working-age men and 62.3 per cent of senior men. Unlike their female counterparts, these men were least likely to have performed these tasks by themselves.

For men with disabilities, the presence of other people in the household brought assistance with household chores,

Figure 6.11

Women and men <u>aged 15 to 64</u> with disabilities, by who performed meal preparation and by living arrangements,1991

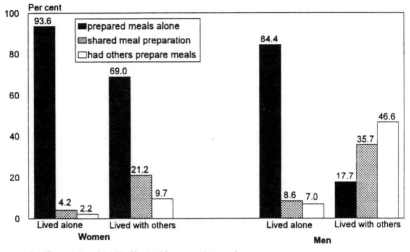

See "Presentation of data" in Chapter 1 for assumptions used.

Figure 6.12

Women and men <u>aged 65 and older</u> with disabilities, by who performed meal preparation and by living arrangements, 1991

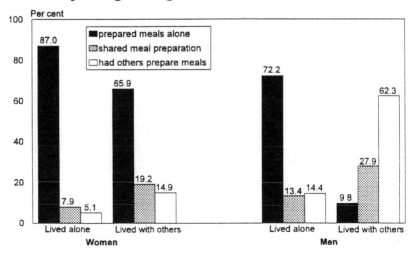

See "Presentation of data" in Chapter 1 for assumptions used.

and this help usually involved having someone else perform the chores entirely. For women, the presence of other people in the household meant only a slightly greater likelihood of having assistance with such tasks. The vast majority of women with disabilities who lived with others performed their domestic tasks alone. This is, no doubt, a reflection of the division of labour that is typically found within the general population, where women bear the primary responsibility for basic household chores.

Household chores and severity of the disability

For women, the severity of their disability was a major factor in whether they had others perform domestic tasks for them. For example, among those who had meals prepared entirely by others, a much higher proportion of women than men had severe disabilities. Among working-age men with disabilities who had their meals prepared for them, 54.5 per cent had a mild disability, 28.7 per cent had a moderate disability and 16.7 per cent had a severe disability (Figure 6.13). Among their female counterparts, however, only 37.8

Figure 6.13

Women and men <u>aged 15-64</u> with disabilities who had <u>meals prepared</u> for them by others, by severity of disability, 1991

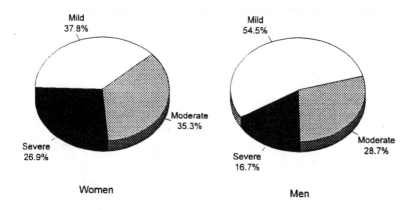

See "Presentation of data" in Chapter 1 for assumptions used.

per cent had a mild disability, 35.3 per cent had a moderate disability and 26.9 per cent had a severe disability.[12]

These differences were even more pronounced among seniors with disabilities. Among women aged 65 and older who had their meals prepared for them, only 14.3 per cent had a mild disability; among the men, the figure was 41.4 per cent (Figure 6.14); 55.7 per cent of the women had a severe disability, compared to only 28.6 per cent of the men.[13]

Figure 6.14

Women and men <u>aged 65 and older</u> with disabilities who had <u>meals prepared</u> for them by others, by severity of disability, 1991

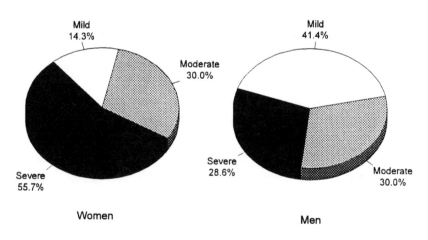

Women

Men

See "Presentation of data" in Chapter 1 for assumptions used.

12. Among all working-age men with disabilities, 57.3 per cent had a mild disability, 29 per cent had a moderate disability and 13.7 per cent had a severe disability. Among all working-age women with disabilities, 51.5 per cent had a mild disability, 34.1 per cent had a moderate disability and 14.5 per cent had a severe disability.

13. Among all senior men with disabilities, 43.7 per cent had a mild disability, 34.5 per cent had a moderate disability and 21.8 per cent had a severe disability. Among all senior women with disabilities, 36.5 per cent had a mild disability, 35.7 per cent had a moderate disability and 27.8 per cent had a severe disability.

Figure 6.15

Women and men <u>aged 15-64</u> with disabilities who had <u>everyday housework</u> done for them by others, by severity of disability, 1991

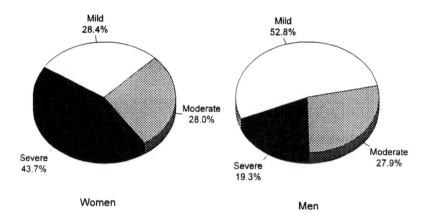

See "Presentation of data" in Chapter 1 for assumptions used.

Figure 6.16

Women and men <u>aged 65 and older</u> with disabilities who had <u>everyday housework</u> done for them by others, by severity of disability, 1991

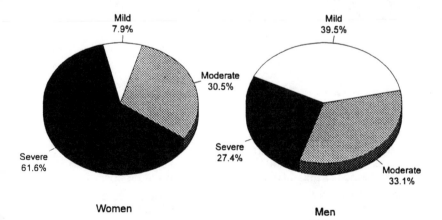

See "Presentation of data" in Chapter 1 for assumptions used.

These sex differences in severity level were even more pronounced in the performance of everyday housework. Among working-age men with disabilities who had someone else do their housework, 19.3 per cent had a severe disability; among their female counterparts, this figure was more than double, at 43.7 per cent (Figure 6.15). The pattern was even more pronounced among seniors who had someone else do their housework for them, where only 7.9 per cent of the women had a mild disability and 61.6 per cent had a severe disability. Among their male counterparts who had their everyday housework done for them, 39.5 per cent had a mild disability and 27.4 per cent had a severe disability (Figure 6.16).

Discussion

As was described in Chapter 1, a handicap is produced by the interaction of a disability with environmental factors. When comparing women and men with disabilities, it is important to remember that while they may live side by side, they often face very different environmental situations. Cultural attitudes about the division of domestic labour can strongly influence the nature of the barriers that women and men with disabilities face. Similar to women in the general population, women with disabilities assume a disproportionate share of the domestic labour within their households, and this can represent a barrier to their labour force participation. For women with disabilities, however, this is yet another barrier that will interact with their disability.

The responsibility for preschool-aged children reduced the likelihood of being in the paid labour force both for women with and without disabilities. Compounding this, women with disabilities also had a greater likelihood of being lone parents, which further decreased the likelihood of their labour force participation and increased their likelihood of living in poverty. For example, women aged 25 to 44 with disabilities were twice as likely as women without disabilities and over five times as likely as men with disabilities to be lone parents. This tendency toward lone parenthood was

primarily due to the greater likelihood of women with
disabilities to be divorced, separated or widowed.

Both women and men with disabilities had increased
labour force participation rates and lower poverty rates when
they lived with others in the household. It would appear that
labour force participation was facilitated by the presence of
these other people, however, the effects of this were much
stronger for men than for women, probably because of the
sex differences in the division of domestic labour within most
households.

Regardless of whether they lived with others or not,
women with disabilities were responsible for the bulk of the
domestic chores like meal preparation and everyday
housework, and they typically performed such chores
without assistance from anyone else. Despite this, women
who lived with others were slightly more likely (than those
who lived alone) to share the responsibility for domestic
chores, and this seemed to facilitate their labour force
participation. Seldom did women with disabilities have
someone else perform household tasks for them, and when
they did, it was typically because of the severity of their
disability. Women were likely to have someone else perform
these tasks only when they had a more severe disability.

Quite a different pattern existed for men with disabilities
when it came to the responsibility for domestic chores by
living arrangements. When men with disabilities lived alone,
they tended to perform domestic chores for themselves,
although not to the same degree as their female
counterparts. When they lived with others, however, the
men were the most likely to have had someone else perform
these household chores for them – regardless of the
severity of their disability. For the men, assistance with
domestic labour seemed to hinge upon their living
arrangements and the division of labour that had been
established within their household, not upon the severity of
their disability. Moreover, while having assistance with
domestic tasks led to greater labour force participation rates

for both sexes, men with disabilities benefited more from this help (and they were more likely to get it).

For women with disabilities, some domestic labour patterns tended to vary by age. In particular, the experiences of young women were a bit different from that of older women. They were less likely to have children and the responsibilities that go along with them, yet they were also more likely to have assistance with domestic chores. It was not surprising, therefore, that these young women typically had very high labour force participation rates relative to their male counterparts.

About two-thirds of women aged 15 to 24 with disabilities still resided with one or both parents. They may be unique in that they may be less likely than the older women to fall into the established patterns for the division of domestic labour. Or, they may follow in the footsteps of these older women once they enter the next phase of their life cycle by going out on their own and forming their own families.

These young women were unique in other ways as well. While all groups of women with disabilities tended to have higher educational attainments than their male counterparts, women in the youngest age group were gaining on their male counterparts at a faster pace. Among those who were no longer pursuing their education, the young women were much more likely than the young men to have completed post-secondary credentials. As well, young women in this age group were more likely to still be pursuing their education, suggesting that even greater gains might be evident once they advanced through their school-age years. All of these differences contributed to the closing of the sex gap in participation rates among those aged 15 to 24. Again, it remains to be seen whether these young women represent a unique group in history or whether this is merely evidence of sex differences in the early stages of the life cycle.

Regardless of the future for these young women, it is clear that in the past, the domestic labour challenge has presented significant barriers to labour force participation and has contributed to increased poverty for many women with disabilities. Like women in the general population, women with disabilities are likely to face other barriers in the labour market, even beyond those discussed here. Just as cultural attitudes toward sex roles are reflected in the division of domestic labour in the home, they are likely to have an impact on the opportunities available to women with disabilities outside the home, in the paid labour market.

Chapter 7

Final Notes

Having a job provides the best protection against poverty for persons with disabilities. While the same might be said about the population in general, persons with disabilities face far greater challenges in getting a job. There is ample evidence that persons with disabilities are willing to join the labour force and that they have the potential for paid employment. Yet many remain outside the labour force, often providing unpaid labour in the home and in the volunteer workforce.

The labour market can be an unfriendly environment for persons with disabilities. Without special accommodations in the workplace, some disabilities unnecessarily result in handicaps to labour force participation. Attitudinal barriers can also produce handicaps when employers focus on disabilities rather than abilities. As well, the personal environment can have an impact on employment for persons with disabilities. For example, it appears that those who have assistance with basic household tasks – such as help with meal preparation, everyday household chores and grocery shopping – are more likely to be in the labour market and be employed than those who do not. This creates a particular disadvantage for women with disabilities since they are much less likely than their male counterparts to have assistance with these tasks.

A lack of other personal supports and services can present additional barriers to employment. For some people, assistance with supports such as subsidized medication, assistive devices and special transportation is linked to the receipt of social assistance. This often creates a trap – the very supports and services that would make employment possible are provided only in the absence of employment. As long as these disability-related personal supports and services are linked to income support programs, the programs themselves can result in handicaps to labour force participation.

Some income support programs for persons with disabilities include the concept of "unemployability," which further detracts from their effectiveness. This assumption about the unemployability of persons with disabilities – which, unfortunately, has been woven into our culture and our social policies – is based on two misconceptions. First, it assumes that a disability alone can prevent a person from working; second, it assumes that disability is a static state. In fact, it is the combination of a disability and the environment in which it is experienced that creates an employment handicap.

So when we think in terms of the employability of persons with disabilities, we must consider both sides of the equation – the disability and the environment. As long as the environment contains barriers, persons with disabilities will face a greater challenge when seeking employment. But environments can change, making employment possible for some. And just as environments can change, so too can disabilities. While some persons with disabilities continue to have the same degree of functional limitation over time, many others experience fluctuations in the severity of their disability, or the presence of it. The interaction between a disability, or the presence of it. The interaction between a disability and the environment is a dynamic one. Policies that do not take this dynamic interaction into account will fail to recognize the full productive potential of persons with disabilities.

Persons with disabilities benefit economically from higher levels of education and from job training – just as people do in the general population. And, as is often the case, the foundation for education and training is laid at a young age. In the first chapter, the example of a young boy being integrated into a daycare centre was used to demonstrate the model of the handicaps creation process. In the example, the young boy had a speaking disability, but the disability had not led to a communication handicap because he had been provided with technical aids which allowed for non-oral communication. Without such communication, the child's opportunities for education later in life could have been limited. Other problems or barriers in his environment – like the inaccessibility of the furniture, games and activities, and the negative attitude of some staff – interacted with the child's disability to create physical and social handicaps for him which could negatively affect his educational opportunities in the future.

While this book deals with adults with disabilities, the example of the child reminds us that the effects of environmental barriers accumulate over time. Certainly for persons whose disability began early in life, the barriers they face as adults are rooted in those faced in childhood. Handicaps with respect to communication, social interaction and learning that are created early in life can limit educational opportunities throughout life – thereby limiting an adult's labour force opportunities. The availability of a range of special education programs, inclusive regular programs, and accessible schools can translate into greater economic security for persons with disabilities in the future.

The rate of disability among Canadians of all ages increased from 13.2 per cent in 1986 to 15.5 per cent in

1991. Despite speculation to the contrary, this was not simply due to the fact that Canada's population is aging and disability rates increase with age – the impact of our aging population on disability rates will only be evident in the years to come. In fact, the greatest increases in disability rates between 1986 and 1991 were among the younger age groups. Over time, it is young people – with and without disabilities – who will be called upon to provide the base of support for a growing population of seniors. We cannot afford to waste their potential because we have adhered to old attitudes and maintained environments that exclude persons with disabilities from the labour force.

Finally, we need to recognize that some persons with disabilities face greater challenges than others. Women with disabilities, those with severe disabilities, and those with mental/learning disabilities face some of the greatest labour force barriers of all. We must also realize that there are some persons for whom no accommodation, assistive devices, medication, or other supports presently exist which could facilitate their labour force participation. For these individuals, there must be adequate income support programs and services to permit their full citizenship.

Persons with disabilities are a diverse group with diverse needs – yet what they do have in common is a great deal of untapped potential. And as we prepare to enter a new century, with governments at all levels making spending cuts, we must remember that in order for persons with disabilities to realize their full potential for self-sufficiency, we must create environments that do not turn their disabilities into handicaps.

References

Avard, Denise. *Children and Youth with Disabilities in Canada*. Ottawa: Statistics Canada, 1994.

Basset, Penny. "Declining female labour force participation" in *Perspectives on Labour and Income*, Summer 1994, Vol. 6, No. 2: 36-39.

Boschen, Kathryn A. *Variables Affecting Independent Living for Persons with Physical Disabilities*. Ottawa: National Welfare Grants Program, Human Resources Development Canada, 1995.

Canadian Institute of Child Health. *The Health of Canada's Children: A CICH Profile*. Ottawa: CICH, 1994.

Canadian Society for the ICIDH and Quebec Committee on the ICIDH. *ICIDH International Network*, June 1991, Volume 4, Nos.1-2.

Chapireau, Francois. *The conceptual framework of the international classification of impairments, disabilities and handicaps (ICIDH)*. Strasbourg: Council of Europe, Publishing and Documentation Service, 1992.

Cohen, Gary L. "Disabled Workers" in *Perspectives on Labour and Income*, Winter 1989, Vol. 1, No. 3: 31-38.

Furrie, Adele D. *Comparison of the Results from the 1986 Census and the Health and Activity Limitation Survey for Persons with Disabilities Residing in Households*. Ottawa: Statistics Canada, 1989.

Hill, Jennifer Leigh. "Adults with Disabilities: Barriers to Post-Secondary Education" in *Youth in Transition, Perspectives on Research and Policy*. Edited by Burt Galaway and Joe Hudson. Toronto: Thompson Educational Publishing Inc., 1996.

Hum, Derek, and Wayne Simpson. *The Economic Well-being and Labour Market Activity of Persons with Disabilities in Canada*. Ottawa: Employment Equity Data Program, Housing, Family and Social Statistics Division, Statistics Canada, 1993.

_____. *Sources of Income of Persons with Disabilities in Canada*. Ottawa: Employment Equity Data Program, Housing, Family and Social Statistics Division, Statistics Canada, 1994.

Human Resources Development Canada (HRDC). *Improving Social Security in Canada, Persons with Disabilities: A Supplementary Paper*. Ottawa: Supply and Services Canada, 1994.

Ison, Terence G. *Compensation Systems for Injury and Disease: The Policy Choices*. Toronto: Butterworths, 1994.

McDowell, Ian. *A Disability Score for The Health and Activity Limitation Survey*. Ottawa: Statistics Canada, 1988.

Federal/Provincial/Territorial Review of Services Affecting Canadians with Disabilities. *Pathway to Integration: Final Report, Mainstream 1992.* Ottawa: Report to Ministers of Social Services on the Federal/Provincial/Territorial Review of Services Affecting Canadians with Disabilities, 1993.

Muszynski, Leon. "An idea whose time has come. Universal disability insurance should replace an irrational and unfair system" in *Perception*, Spring 1989, Vol. 13, No. 2: 55-56.

_____. "The Need for a Comprehensive and Integrated Disability Income System" in *Compass*, December 1990, Vol. 2, Issue 8: 32-35.

Nessner, Katherine. "Profile of Canadians with Disabilities" in *Canadian Social Trends*, Autumn 1990a, No. 18: 2-6.

_____. "Children with Disabilities" in *Canadian Social Trends*, Winter 1990b, No. 19: 18-21.

Oderkirk, Jillian. "Disabilities Among Children" in *Canadian Social Trends*, Winter 1993, No. 31: 22-25.

Ontario Ministry of Community and Social Services. *Transitions. Report of the Social Assistance Review Committee.* Prepared for the Ontario Ministry of Community and Social Services. Toronto: Queen's Printer for Ontario, 1988.

Roeher Institute. *Income Insecurity: The Disability Income System in Canada.* Toronto: The Roeher Institute, 1988.

_____. *Poor Places: Disability-Related Residential and Support Services.* Toronto: The Roeher Institute, 1990.

_____. *Comprehensive Disability Income Security Reform.* Toronto: The Roeher Institute, 1992.

_____ . *Direct Dollars: A Study of Individualized Funding in Canada.* Toronto: The Roeher Institute, 1993a.

_____ . *Nothing Personal: The Need for Personal Supports in Canada.* Toronto: The Roeher Institute, 1993b.

_____ . *On Target?* Toronto: The Roeher Institute, 1993c.

_____ . *The Canadian Disability Resource Program: Offsetting Costs of Disability and Assuring Access to Disability-Related Supports.* Toronto: The Roeher Institute, 1994.

_____ . *Disability-Related Supports: Costs and Delivery System for Selected Provinces.* Toronto: The Roeher Institute, 1995a.

_____ . *Harm's Way: The Many Faces of Violence and Abuse against Persons with Disabilities in Canada.* Toronto: The Roeher Institute, 1995b.

Ross, David P. and E. Richard Shillington. *A Profile of the Canadian Volunteer.* Ottawa: National Voluntary Organizations, 1989.

_____ . *An Economic Profile of Persons with Disabilities in Canada.* Ottawa: Secretary of State of Canada, 1990.

Ross, David P., E. Richard Shillington and Clarence Lochhead. *The Canadian Fact Book on Poverty – 1994.* Ottawa: Canadian Council on Social Development, 1994.

Shain, Alan. "Employment of People with Disabilities" in *Canadian Social Trends*, Autumn 1995, No. 38: 8-13.

Schellenberg, Grant. *The Road to Retirement: Demographic and Economic Changes in the 90s.* Ottawa: Centre for International Statistics, Canadian Council on Social Development, 1994.

Standing Committee on Human Rights and the Status of Disabled Persons. *The Grand Design: Achieving the "Open House" Vision.* Minutes of the Proceedings of the Standing Committee on Human Rights and the Status of Disabled Persons, Issue No. 50, Meetings Nos. 79 to 84, 1995.

Statistics Canada. "1991 Health and Activity Limitation Survey" in *The Daily*, Tuesday, October 13, 1992. Ottawa: Statistics Canada, 1992.

_____ . "1991 Health and Activity Limitation Survey: Employment and Education" in *The Daily*, Tuesday, July 27, 1993. Ottawa: Statistics Canada, 1993a.

_____ . *Adults with Disabilities: Their Employment and Education Characteristics.* Ottawa: Industry, Science and Technology, 1993b.

_____ . *Selected Characteristics of Persons with Disabilities Residing in Households.* Ottawa: Industry, Science and Technology, 1994.

_____ . *A Portrait of Persons with Disabilities.* Ottawa: Industry, Science and Technology; 1995.

World Health Organization. *International Classification of Impairments, Disabilities and Handicaps.* Geneva: World Health Organization, 1980.

Appendix A

Screening questions
from the 1991 HALS

[also indicates which questions were
included in the 1989-90 LMAS]

A1   Do you have any difficulty hearing what is said in a
       conversation with one other person? [Not in LMAS]

A2   Do you have any difficulty hearing what is said in a
       group conversation with at least three other people?
       [In LMAS]

A4   Do you have any difficulty seeing ordinary newsprint
       with glasses or contact lenses, if usually worn?
       [In LMAS]

A5   Do you have any difficulty clearly seeing the face of someone across a room (from 4 metres or 12 feet) with glasses or contact lenses, if usually worn? [Not in LMAS]

A7   Do you have any difficulty speaking and being understood? [In LMAS]

A8   Do you have any difficulty walking 350 metres or 400 yard without resting (about three city blocks, about half a kilometre or a quarter of a mile)? [In LMAS as follows: Do you have any trouble walking 400 yards/400 metres without resting (about three city blocks)?]

A9   Do you have any difficulty walking up and down a flight of stairs (about 12 steps)? [In LMAS]

A10   Do you have any difficulty carrying an object of 4.5 kg for 10 metres or 10 pounds for 30 feet (for example, carrying a bag of groceries)? [In LMAS]

A11   Do you have any difficulty moving from one room to another? [Not in LMAS]

A12   Do you have any difficulty standing for more than 20 minutes? [In LMAS]

A13   When standing, do you have any difficulty bending down and picking up an object from the floor (for example, a shoe)? [In LMAS]

A14   Do you have any difficulty dressing and undressing yourself? [Not in LMAS]

A15   Do you have any difficulty getting in and out of bed? [Not in LMAS]

A16   Do you have any difficulty cutting your own toenails? (That is, is it physically difficult for you to cut your own toenails?) [Not in LMAS]

A17   Do you have any difficulty using your fingers to grasp or handle (such as using pliers or scissors)? [In LMAS]

A18   Do you have any difficulty reaching in any direction (for example, above your head)? [In LMAS]

A19   Do you have any difficulty cutting your own food? [Not in LMAS]

A20i   Because of a long-term physical condition or health problem (that is, one that has lasted or is expected to last six months or more), are you limited in the kind or amount of activity you can do at home? [In LMAS]

A20ii   Because of a long-term physical condition or health problem (that is, one that has lasted or is expected to last six months or more), are you limited in the kind or amount of activity you can do at school? [In LMAS]

A20iii   Because of a long-term physical condition or health problem (that is, one that has lasted or is expected to last six months or more), are you limited in the kind or amount of activity you can do at work? [In LMAS]

A20iv   Because of a long-term physical condition or health problem (that is, one that has lasted or is expected to last six months or more), are you limited in the kind or amount of activity you can do in other activities, such as travel, sport or leisure? [In LMAS]

A21   From time to time, everyone has difficulty remembering the name of a familiar person, or learning something new, or they experience moments of confusion. However, do you have any ongoing difficulty with your ability to remember or learn? [In LMAS]

A24a Has a teacher or health professional (such as a doctor, nurse, social worker or counsellor) ever told you or your family that you have a learning disability (such as dyslexia, a perceptual handicap, attention problems or hyperactivity)? [Not in LMAS]

A24b In the past, persons who had some difficulty learning were often told they had a mental handicap or that they were developmentally delayed or mentally retarded. Has anyone ever used these words to describe you? [Not in LMAS]

A25i Because of a long-term emotional, psychological, nervous or psychiatric condition (that is, one that has lasted or is expected to last six months or more), are you limited in the kind or amount of activity you can do at home? [In LMAS]

A25ii Because of a long-term emotional, psychological, nervous or psychiatric condition (that is, one that has lasted or is expected to last six months or more), are you limited in the kind or amount of activity you can do at school? [In LMAS]

A25iii Because of a long-term emotional, psychological, nervous or psychiatric condition (that is, one that has lasted or is expected to last six months or more), are you limited in the kind or amount of activity you can do at work? [In LMAS]

A25iv Because of a long-term emotional, psychological, nervous or psychiatric condition (that is, one that has lasted or is expected to last six months or more), are you limited in the kind or amount of activity you can do in other activities, such as travel, sport or leisure? [In LMAS]

A29ai Do you feel limited by the fact that a health professional has labelled you with a specific mental health condition, whether you agree with this label or not – at home? [Not in LMAS]

A29aii Do you feel limited by the fact that a health professional has labelled you with a specific mental health condition, whether you agree with this label or not – at school? [Not in LMAS]

A29aiii Do you feel limited by the fact that a health professional has labelled you with a specific mental health condition, whether you agree with this label or not – at work? [Not in LMAS]

A29aiv Do you feel limited by the fact that a health professional has labelled you with a specific mental health condition, whether you agree with this label or not – in other activities, such as travel, sport or leisure? [Not in LMAS]

Appendix B

Supporting tables

Table B.1

Labour force status of persons with disabilities by sex, 1986 and 1991

	Women		
	1986	**1991**	
Labour force status	**%**	**%**	Number
Employed	31.2	40.7	473,000
Unemployed	6.4	7.8	90,000
Total in labour force (participation rates)	37.6	48.5	563,000
Not in labour force	62.4	51.5	598,000
Total ILF & NILF	100.0	100.0	1,161,000

	Men		
	1986	**1991**	
Labour force status	**%**	**%**	Number
Employed	50.8	55.8	634,000
Unemployed	8.4	8.4	96,000
Total in labour force (participation rates)	59.2	64.2	730,000
Not in labour force	40.8	35.8	407,000
Total ILF & NILF	100.0	100.0	1,136,000

See "Presentation of data" in Chapter 1 for assumptions used.

Table B.2

Persons with disabilities, highest level of education by sex, 1991

	Women		Men	
Education	%	Number	%	Number
Primary	18.0	209,000	21.4	243,000
Some secondary	28.2	327,000	25.7	292,000
Secondary	15.2	176,000	11.8	134,000
Trades	8.0	93,000	16.0	181,000
Some post-secondary	10.5	122,000	9.8	111,000
Non-university post-sec.	14.6	169,000	9.1	104,000
University	5.6	64,000	6.2	70,000
Total	100.0	1,160,000	100.0	1,135,000

See "Presentation of data" in Chapter 1 for assumptions used.

Table B.3

Labour force participation rates* for persons with disabilities,
by highest level of education completed and by whether the
underlying condition was present before or after completion
of education, 1991

	Condition present before	
Highest level of education completed	Participation rate (%)	Number
Less than high school completed	53.7	178,000
High school completed	71.7	116,000
Trades certificate	75.3	49,000
Post-secondary school completed	82.2	120,000
All levels	67.9	462,000

	Condition present after	
Highest level of education completed	Participation rate (%)	Number
Less than high school completed	43.0	641,000
High school completed	58.5	300,000
Trades certificate	64.8	188,000
Post-secondary school completed	63.1	212,000
All levels	52.7	1,341,000

*employed or unemployed
See "Presentation of data" in Chapter 1 for assumptions used.

Table B.4

Labour force participation rates* for women and men with and without disabilities, by living arrangements, 1991

Women

Living arrangements	With disabilities		Without disabilities	
	Participation rate (%)	Number	Participation rate (%)	Number
Lived alone	43.5	136,000	82.5	460,000
Lived with others	49.7	997,000	72.7	7,401,000
Total	48.9	1,133,000	73.3	7,861,000
% Lived alone	12.0		5.8	

Men

Living arrangements	With disabilities		Without disabilities	
	Participation rate (%)	Number	Participation rate (%)	Number
Lived alone	59.1	126,000	91.5	515,000
Lived with others	66.4	962,000	88.4	7,295,000
Total	65.5	1,088,000	88.6	7,810,000
% Lived alone	11.6		6.6	

*employed or unemployed
See "Presentation of data" in Chapter 1 for assumptions used.

Table B.5

Employment earnings for persons with disabilities working full-time with some earnings, by age, 1991

	Employment earnings					
Age	$1-9,999	$10,000-$14,999	$15,000-$24,999	$25,000-$34,999	$35,000+	Total %
15-24	48.0%	17.1%	25.4%	8.3%	*	100
25-44	14.0%	10.9%	19.5%	25.9%	29.6%	100
45-64	14.7%	9.2%	20.5%	21.2%	34.5%	100
Total	17.2%	10.7%	20.4%	22.5%	29.2%	100

Age	Total number
15-24	68,000
25-44	394,000
45-64	322,000
Total	783,000

*sample size too low to yield stable estimates
See "Presentation of data" in Chapter 1 for assumptions used.

Table B.6

Employment earnings for persons with disabilities working full-time with some earnings, by educational attainment, 1991

	Employment earnings					
Education	$1-$9,999	$10,000-$14,999	$15,000-$24,999	$25,000-$34,999	$35,000+	Total %
Less than high school	21.8%	15.2%	19.6%	21.6%	21.8%	100
High school completed	17.5%	9.6%	28.4%	21.5%	22.9%	100
Trades	14.5%	7.3%	15.4%	30.4%	32.4%	100
Post-secondary	12.7%	8.2%	16.2%	19.4%	43.5%	100
Total	17.2%	10.7%	20.4%	22.5%	29.2%	100

Education	Number*
Less than high school	256,000
High school completed	208,000
Trades	126,000
Post-secondary	193,000
Total	783,000

*Numbers may not add up due to rounding.
See "Presentation of data" in Chapter 1 for assumptions used.

Table B.7

Employment earnings for persons with disabilities working full-time with some earnings, by severity, 1991

	Employment earnings					
Severity	$1-$9,999	$10,000-$14,999	$15,000-$24,999	$25,000-$34,999	$35,000+	Total %
Mild	17.2%	9.7%	20.4%	22.0%	30.7%	100
Moderate	17.1%	14.0%	19.8%	23.3%	25.8%	100
Severe	18.7%	9.8%	23.9%	26.4%	21.2%	100
Total	17.2%	10.7%	20.4%	22.5%	29.2%	100

Severity	Number*
Mild	565,000
Moderate	183,000
Severe	35,000
Total	783,000

*Numbers may not add up due to rounding.
See "Presentation of data" in Chapter 1 for assumptions used.

Table B.8

Composite measure of future work potential for women and men with disabilities not in the labour force*, by severity, 1991

	Women		
	Work potential		**Total**
Severity	Number	%	
Mild	99,000	42.7	231,000
Moderate	68,000	29.0	234,000
Severe	29,000	22.0	132,000
Total	196,000	32.7	598,000

	Men		
	Work potential		**Total**
Severity	Number	%	
Mild	45,000	33.8	133,000
Moderate	47,000	28.3	166,000
Severe	22,000	20.4	108,000
Total	114,000	28.0	407,000

*These individuals: (1) were still students; (2) were performing volunteer work requiring skills that were useful in paid labour market; (3) intended to look for work in the next six months; (4) had not worked for pay in at least five years but had looked within the last five years and had been turned down because of disability; or (5) had not worked for pay in at least five years but had looked for work without success during the last two years. See "Presentation of data" in Chapter 1 for assumptions used.

Table B.9

Poverty rates for persons with disabilities* by labour force status, 1991

	Seniors	Employed	Unemployed	NILF*	Total
			Labour force status		
No. poor	263,000	145,000	43,000	295,000	746,000
% poor	22.1	13.4	23.9	31.0	21.9
Total number	1,191,000	1,083,000	180,000	951,000	3,405,000

*not in the labour force
See "Presentation of data" in Chapter 1 for assumptions used.

Table B.10

Poverty rates for persons with disabilities by age group and sex, 1991

	15-24 yrs	25-44 yrs	45-64 yrs	65 + yrs	Total
Women					
No. poor	27,000	111,000	136,000	183,000	457,000
% poor	20.4	25.0	24.5	26.6	25.1
Total number	130,000	443,000	556,000	689,000	1,818,000
Men					
No. poor	22,000	83,000	104,000	79,000	288,000
% poor	18.3	20.0	19.0	15.8	18.2
Total number	123,000	414,000	548,000	502,000	1,587,000

See "Presentation of data" in Chapter 1 for assumptions used.

Table B.11

Poverty rates for persons with disabilities, for those with some income from selected sources, 1991

	No. poor	% poor	Total no.
Social Assistance	157,000	66.2	238,000
CPP/QPP Disability	61,000	27.4	223,000
Workers' Compensation	19,000	14.2	137,000

See "Presentation of data" in Chapter 1 for assumptions used.

Table B.12

Labour force status of women aged 25 to 44 with disabilities, by presence of dependent children, 1991

Dependent children	Labour force status: number			
	Employed	Unemployed	NILF	Total
None	77,000	14,000	54,000	146,000
Children under 6	45,000	11,000	39,000	96,000
Children over 5	107,000	19,000	70,000	196,000
Total	229,000	45,000	164,000	438,000

Dependent children	Labour force status: per cent			
	Employed	Unemployed	NILF	Total
None	53.0	9.9	37.1	100
Children under 6	47.3	11.5	41.3	100
Children over 5	54.4	9.9	35.7	100
Total	52.4	10.2	37.4	100

See "Presentation of data" in Chapter 1 for assumptions used.

Appendix C

Regression analysis:
Earnings and selected variables

The relationships between earnings and selected variables that were described in Chapter 3 can also be summarized using multiple regression analysis. Regression analysis is a more refined tool than the simple cross-tabulation analysis used in Chapter 3 (and the other chapters). It can be used to measure the effects of a number of variables on earnings.

While the cross-tabulation analysis focusses on the effects of a number of variables on earnings, it does not allow for a comparison of the magnitude of the effect of each variable with that of the others. However, by reducing the effects of all variables to a single equation, regression analysis allows for such a comparison. It also provides a measure of the effect of each variable "net" of the effect of the other variables; in other words, it allows us to control for the effects of the other variables in the equation.

A number of different variables were considered for their possible impact on earnings. The final model included those variables that had a statistically significant relationship with earnings. The following section summarizes the main findings of the regression analysis and provides more details about the model itself.

The results of the regression analysis

The results of the regression analysis reveal that the most important factors in determining the earnings of persons with disabilities in 1991 were education, occupation, training, sex and age. Of these variables, education is considered the single most important because it exerted strong direct and indirect effects on the earnings of persons with disabilities. Higher education enabled some people to obtain higher-paying occupations and led to greater opportunities for training, which in turn led to higher earnings. The following summarizes the major findings from this analysis:

- Persons with disabilities who had a high school diploma had slightly higher earnings than those who had not completed their high school education. For men, an even bigger boost to their earnings was provided by a trades certificate. For women, however, a trades certificate actually seemed to have a negative effect on their earnings. For both sexes, the greatest earnings premium came from obtaining post-secondary (non-trade) credentials. Separate analysis indicated that this level of education led to higher levels of training and to higher-paying occupations.

- Two occupational categories provided substantially higher earnings opportunities for persons with disabilities: supervisors/forewomen and foremen, and professionals and managers. Although only 5.3 per cent of persons with disabilities working full-time were employed in the former category, nearly 22 per cent worked in the latter.

- For persons with disabilities, having work-related training provided a significant boost to their employment income. Separate analysis reveals that those who had post-secondary education were the most likely to have had such training.

- Large earnings "penalties" were experienced by women with disabilities. Women who had trades certification or were employed in blue-collar work suffered an even greater penalty.

- Young people (aged 15 to 24) with disabilities also experienced a large earnings penalty.

- Having a more severe disability and a need for special transportation led to lower levels of earnings. However, once all other factors were taken into consideration, the effects of these two variables were surprisingly modest. It is important to remember that these two variables affect earnings directly and indirectly. Separate analysis reveals, for example, that severity level and a need for special transportation both influence a person's occupational opportunities and their likelihood of having work-related training – both of which, in turn, affect earnings.

The model

The unstandardized regression coefficients for the regression of earnings on selected variables for persons with disabilities can be found in Table C.1. The coefficients for two models are also summarized in the table. The first model represents the full equation used to draw the conclusions previously summarized. The second model is similar to the first, except that training and the occupational variables are not included. The two equations allow us to see how the coefficients for the education variables change when work-related training and occupational category are controlled – suggesting that there was an indirect effect of education on earnings through training and occupation. This can also be seen in the cross-tabular analysis, as well (as outlined in Chapter 3).

As summarized here, the variables explained just over one-quarter of the variation in earnings of persons with disabilities. Some of the methodological details of the model are described below:

Table C.1

Coefficients for regression of earnings on selected variables for persons aged 15 to 64 with disabilities working full-time, 1991

Variables	Model 1 B	Model 2 B
Completed high school	1772 *	3352 *
Completed trades credentials	2749 *	5397 *
Trades x woman (Interaction)	-6242 *	-7321 *
Post-secondary credentials	4375 *	8422 *
Training	5433 *	
Woman	-6698 *	-8099 *
Aged 15 to 24	-11832 *	-13608 *
Aged 45 to 64	1844 *	1867 *
Moderate or severe disability	-1387 *	-1680 *
Required accessible transportation	-265 *	-506 *
Semi-professional/Technical occupation	1717 *	
Supervisor/Forewoman/Foreman	6527 *	
Professional/Manager	7860 *	
Blue-collar worker	3394 *	
Blue-collar worker x Woman (Interaction)	-3633 *	
Intercept	22286 *	27239 *
Adjusted R^2	0.28148 *	0.2155 *

* significant at .05 or better
See "Presentation of data" in Chapter 1 for assumptions used.

Measurement of earnings: In order to develop the regression model, the categories of earnings available in the 1991 HALS were converted to dollar values by using the mid-point of each category to represent the entire interval. The open-ended upper category ($35,000 and above) was assigned the value of $45,500; this represents the median earnings of all persons, aged 15 to 64, with earnings over $35,000 in the 1991 Census.

Measurement of educational attainment: Education was entered into the model as a series of dummy variables (completed high school, completed trades certificate and completed post-secondary).

Measurement of occupation: Dummy variables for the following occupational groups were found to be significant and were retained in the final model: semi-professionals/technicians; supervisors/forewomen and foremen; professionals/managers; and blue-collar workers.

Measurement of other variables: Having work-related training was entered as a dummy variable.

Being a woman was also entered into the model as a dummy variable. There were significant interaction effects between being a woman and two of the other variables: blue-collar work and having a trades certificate. Accordingly, these interactions were entered as dummy variables.

Two age categories (15 to 24 and 45 to 64) were entered as dummy variables to capture earnings differences among age groups.

A dummy variable was entered for those with either a moderate or severe disability. To obtain a statistically significant coefficient for severity in the regression model, a single dummy variable was created which represented both moderate and severe disabilities. The use of separate dummy variables for moderate and severe disabilities yielded coefficients of similar size which were not statistically significant.

Having a requirement for accessible transportation was also included as a dummy variable.

Development of the model: A series of regression equations were developed until the model was refined to include only variables with significant effects. Surprisingly, variables such as living alone, number of hours worked above 30 hours per week (only those working at least 30 hours per week were included in the analysis), and requirements for either job redesign or modified hours (for those working 30 hours per week or more) failed to register any significant effects on earnings.

The full model that was developed included the following independent variables:

- **age** (dummy variables for persons aged 15 to 24 and those aged 45 to 64). The reference group was those 25 to 44 years of age.
- **requirement for accessible transportation** (dummy variable)
- **sex** (dummy variable for being a woman)
- **education** (dummy variables for completed high school, trades certification and post-secondary credentials). The reference group was those with less than completed high school.
- **interaction effect of women with trades certification** (dummy variable)
- **severity** (dummy variable for either moderate or severe disability). The reference group was those with mild disabilities.
- **job training** (dummy variable)
- **occupational group** (dummy variables for semi-professional/technical occupations, supervisor/forewomen/foremen, professionals/

managers, and blue-collar workers). The reference group was clerical workers and sales/service workers.

- **an interaction variable for being a woman and a blue-collar worker** (dummy variable)

An additional model was included in an effort to determine more about the nature of the effect of education on earnings. This additional model excluded the training and occupational variables. The coefficients for the education dummy variables were noticeably larger in the model that excluded training and occupational groups – indicating that some of the effect of education on earnings is indirect through training and occupation. Separate cross-tabular analysis confirmed this. Similarly, the coefficients for other variables (such as severity and having a requirement for accessible transportation) were also larger in the model that excluded training and occupation. (Cross-tabular analysis also indicated that severity and a requirement for accessible transportation influenced training and occupation which, in turn, affected earnings.)